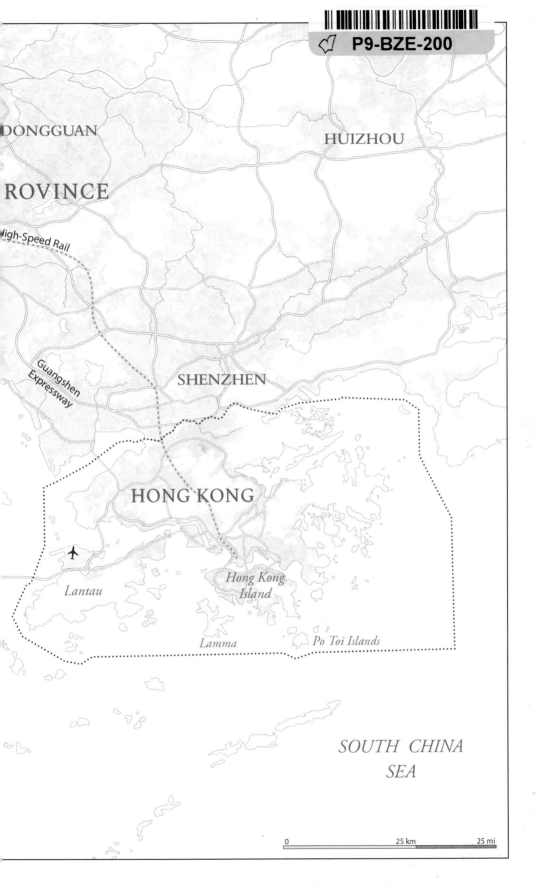

P9-BZE-200

DONGGUAN

HUIZHOU

ROVINCE

High-Speed Rail

Guangshen
Expressway

SHENZHEN

HONG KONG

Lantau

Hong Kong
Island

Lamma

Po Toi Islands

SOUTH CHINA
SEA

0   25 km   25 mi

TODAY HONG KONG, TOMORROW THE WORLD

TODAY
HONG KONG,
TOMORROW
THE WORLD

WHAT CHINA'S CRACKDOWN
REVEALS ABOUT ITS PLANS TO
END FREEDOM EVERYWHERE

MARK L. CLIFFORD

ST. MARTIN'S PRESS
NEW YORK

First published in the United States by St. Martin's Press, an imprint of St. Martin's Publishing Group

TODAY HONG KONG, TOMORROW THE WORLD. Copyright © 2022 by Mark L. Clifford. All rights reserved. Printed in the United States of America. For information, address St. Martin's Publishing Group, 120 Broadway, New York, NY 10271.

www.stmartins.com

All photos courtesy of *Apple Daily*.

Design by Meryl Sussman Levavi

Endpaper and interior maps by Beehive Mapping

The Library of Congress Cataloging-in-Publication Data is available upon request.

ISBN 978-1-250-27917-0 (hardcover)
ISBN 978-1-250-27918-7 (ebook)

Our books may be purchased in bulk for promotional, educational, or business use. Please contact your local bookseller or the Macmillan Corporate and Premium Sales Department at 1-800-221-7945, extension 5442, or by email at MacmillanSpecialMarkets@macmillan.com.

First Edition: 2022

10 9 8 7 6 5 4 3 2 1

For the Hong Kongers demanding the freedom they were promised—to go about their daily lives without the fear of the dawn knock at the door.

And for the *Apple Daily* journalists who fought so hard for liberty.

CONTENTS

No force can block the thirst for freedom that lies within human nature, and some day China, too, will be a nation of laws where human rights are paramount.

—Liu Xiaobo, writer, philosopher, human rights activist, and Nobel Peace Prize laureate; died July 13, 2017, age sixty-one, in Chinese custody

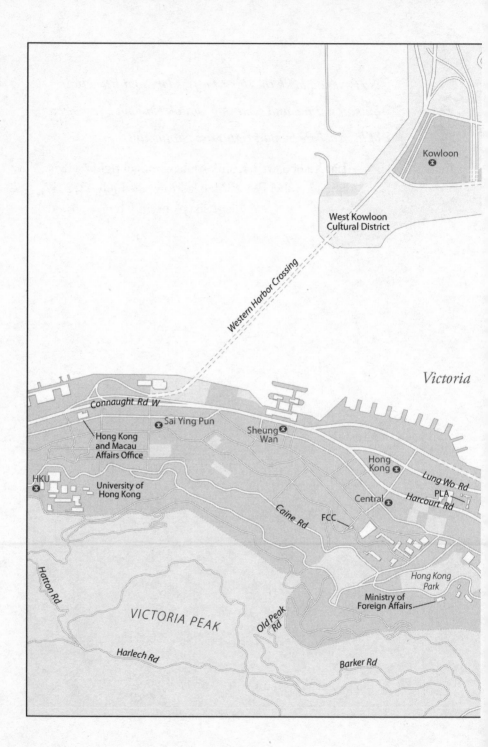

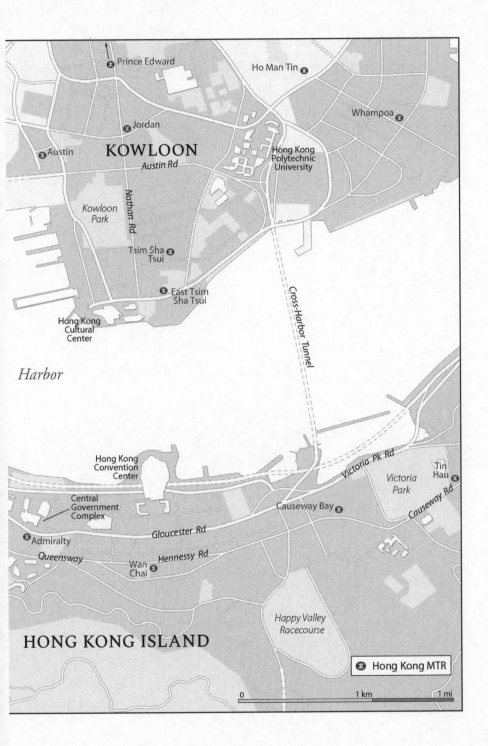

PREFACE

When the People's Republic of China resumed sovereignty over Hong Kong in 1997, it solemnly promised to uphold for fifty years the freedoms that had developed during the British colonial era. Halfway to that milestone, China has instead embarked on a campaign to systematically dismantle the territory's foundational freedoms: of the press, of speech, and of assembly, all underpinned by the rule of law. The party has done this with the help of the Hong Kong government (not democratically elected) and its business elite, who are too shortsighted, too concerned with immediate monetary or status advantages, or too willfully naïve to understand what is at stake.

In 2019, the people of Hong Kong mounted the most sustained challenge to China's rule since Mao Zedong founded the People's Republic in 1949. Hong Kongers had long been pressing Beijing to make good on its promises in the city's mini-constitution for universal suffrage. This wasn't anything radical, simply the right to elect the mayor (known locally as the chief executive) and the city council (the Legislative Council, a largely toothless body that didn't even have the authority to initiate spending bills). Notwithstanding its repeated pre-handover promises, Beijing couldn't stomach the idea of sharing power with anyone who wasn't a "patriot" who "loves the country." Only those politicians who support the Chinese Communist Party (CCP) are eligible for office now, thus disqualifying the overwhelming majority of Hong Kongers who support democracy. Simply put, Beijing's refusal to let Hong Kongers elect their mayor and city council set the stage for conflict. Hong Kong's fight to preserve its freedoms against threats from mainland China is an ongoing test of a democratic society's ability to withstand authoritarian China's pressure. The results to date have been discouraging for anyone who believes in democracy.

The summer of 2019 began with peaceful demonstrations, as some two million people filled the city's streets to oppose a law that would have allowed extradition to mainland China, where Hong Kong's legal protections do not apply and where arbitrary arrests and torture are common. The territory's police responded from the first days with needless violence, setting off an escalating but completely avoidable cycle of confrontation with protesters. There was no attempt to hold the police accountable, let alone to apologize for evident excesses. At the end of a year in which thousands of rounds of tear gas and rubber bullets were fired, one in which protesters invaded and vandalized the Legislative Council, burned subway stations, fired catapult and slingshot projectiles at police, and literally ripped up the city streets, a resounding majority voted for the demonstrators' pro-democracy agenda.

China's Communist Party, angered at its inability to bring Hong Kong to heel and convinced that Western plots to overthrow China lay at the roots of the protests, responded by ushering in an ominous new phase with the July 1, 2020, imposition of a draconian National Security Law and subsequent arrests of dozens of leaders of the democracy movement. Thus began a period of "reeducation" redolent of Mao Zedong's bloody Cultural Revolution, ten years of madness from 1966 to 1976 that saw friends and families on the mainland turn against one another as the revolution devoured its own. In the first year of the National Security Law's introduction in Hong Kong, more than one hundred people, including journalists and political leaders, were arrested under the law's vague and sweeping provisions. Many were denied bail, implicitly deemed guilty by handpicked judges even though it would be a year or more until their trials. Neighbor spied on neighbor, reporting in to a special national security hotline, and kindergarten children goosestepped in fulsome displays of patriotism. Books were stripped from library shelves, movies censored, and the *Apple Daily* newspaper forcibly shuttered. Even the act of laying flowers at the site of a pro-democracy suicide victim was deemed criminal.

❦

What is happening in Hong Kong provides a blueprint for the sorts of tactics that China is increasingly wielding against democratic societies around the globe—its strategy of crushing dissent and silencing independent voices is central to its international playbook. The National Security Law explicitly states that its provisions are global; what China is determined to do in Hong Kong it intends to do next in Taiwan (which it regards as a breakaway province) and, to a lesser degree, in other Asian neighbors like South Korea and Japan, and then around the world, from Africa to Australia. The United States and Europe are not immune; in fact, U.S. citizens have already been targeted. Universities have warned their students that what they say or write in class could be used against them in China, and the State Department has recently urged citizens to reconsider travel to Hong Kong "due to arbitrary enforcement of local laws."

The challenge posed by China has grown since the 2008 global financial crisis. The United States and other open societies relied in large part on China's massive stimulus program to reflate the global economy and, in turn, they muted their longstanding concerns about civil liberties and human rights violations in the People's Republic. For China, the financial crisis revealed the Western financial system, which it had long tried to emulate, as corrupt and showed governments unable to mount coherent reforms. More recently, the erratic response to COVID-19 in liberal democracies has further strengthened China in its belief that illiberal authoritarianism, buttressed by its techno-surveillance state, represents a viable alternative not just for China but for other countries as well.

China's use of a combination of aggressive legal and security policies, aboveground allies, and underground organizations is not just a threat to Hong Kong (where, remarkably, the Chinese Communist Party remains an underground organization). This tiny former British colony is a testing ground for attempts to limit the freedoms of open societies. The Communist destruction of the territory's liberties marks the only time in contemporary history when a totalitarian government has destroyed a free society—has shuttered a free press and ended free speech and freedom of assembly, and curtailed the right to be presumed innocent, the right to a jury trial, and the right to hold private property without the government arbitrarily seizing it. Not since the Soviet takeover of eastern Europe in the late 1940s and the destruction of Shanghai following the 1949 Communist Revolution in China have we seen anything like the devastation Beijing is wreaking in Hong Kong. The free world ignores the tactics on display there at its peril.

This book makes an argument for freedom. The people who lived in late twentieth-century Hong Kong—most of whom were Chinese—developed the territory into one of the most freewheeling and prosperous places in the world. At its best, this process saw Hong Kongers and their colonial rulers combine the best of British institutions (rule of law, and freedom of press, religion, and assembly) with a light-touch government to develop a strong sense of civic freedom—but without democracy, without a chance to choose their leaders at the ballot box. Notwithstanding a belated attempt by Chris Patten, the last colonial governor, to introduce more representative democracy; despite the repeated and clear support for democracy by Hong Kong voters for the three decades since Legislative Council elections began; and contrary to the repeated promises of the incoming Chinese rulers, Hong Kong has been denied democracy. This democratic denial had strong support in both the Chinese and expatriate business communities who were eager to see taxes and wages remain low. For its part, the United States was too preoccupied with Hong Kong's role as a Cold War ally to press for more democracy. Despite ongoing official efforts to tamp down politics, Hong Kongers took advantage of Britain's drawn-out colonial rule—its departure from Hong Kong in 1997 took place almost half a century after it left most other colonies—to develop a unique culture of freedom. That freedom is now being extinguished by a China that permits only the control of one-party rule. This book is about how freedom was nurtured, how it blossomed, and how it now struggles to survive in an increasingly hostile environment.

PART I

"RIVER WATER DOES NOT MIX WITH WELL WATER"

ONE

THE SUMMER OF DEMOCRACY

June 4, 2019—the thirtieth anniversary of the killings near Tiananmen Square, when Chinese troops massacred hundreds of peaceful protesters in Beijing. I am among the crowd; some 150,000 people have gathered in and around Victoria Park, an oasis of grass and sports areas named after the long-serving British queen under whose reign Hong Kong was seized as a war prize, and whose statue still stands on the site. The unusually large turnout reflects heightened political tensions, as a bill that would allow the extradition of criminal suspects to China is expected to be passed by Hong Kong's Legislative Council the following week. There are candles to commemorate the killings, emotionally fraught speeches by mothers of students who were murdered in 1989, exhortations by local democracy activists, and protest songs. The event feels like it is living on borrowed time. Not only are such commemorations banned everywhere else in China, but so is any mention of the anniversary. Even internet posts using the numbers six and four, for June 4, are deleted by censors.

On the subway ride home, I watch a father playing the "tank man" video on his phone for his young son. The grainy footage shows the lone protester who stood in front of, and stopped, a tank on Beijing's Chang'an Avenue right after the Tiananmen killings. The boy is about six years old; he is still wearing his uniform of white shorts and shirt and must have gone straight from school to the commemoration. He watches the video, rapt. His father plays it again. "We have to remember our history," the father tells me by way of explanation. The father, who looks to be in his mid-thirties, would have been about his son's age at the time of the Tiananmen killings.

So began Hong Kong's long summer of democracy. Over the next six months, the city would be convulsed by protests. The campaign to protest a bill allowing extradition to China rapidly transformed into a frontal challenge to the rulers in Beijing. What started as a largely peaceful movement saw more than six thousand demonstrators arrested by year's end, some of them on charges of bomb making and other violent crimes. Police cracked down on the protests brutally during those seven months, firing beanbag rounds and sponge grenades and a staggering sixteen thousand rounds of tear gas and ten thousand rubber bullets. The Chinese Communists alienated yet another generation of Hong Kongers.

In early 2020, unrest ground to a halt as the government used the cover of the COVID-19 pandemic to prohibit large-scale gatherings. The Tiananmen commemoration that year was banned, for the first time ever. Communist Party officials from mainland China moved to assert more direct control over Hong Kong. Midway through 2020, a sweeping National Security Law threatened demonstrators, and their supporters abroad, with stiff sentences that could be be served in mainland prisons for vaguely defined antigovernment offenses. Even protesters holding up blank sheets of paper were arrested and warned that they could be charged with violating the National Security Law. One of those detained said that she was inspired by an old Soviet joke in which a protester is arrested simply for handing out blank sheets of paper in Moscow's Red Square. "You think I didn't know what you wanted to say?" shouts the policeman who detains her.[1] In Hong Kong, the farcical joke has become a tragedy.

How did this happen? How did a beacon of prosperity and freedom, a city of peaceful rallies where fathers stood in vigil with their school-age children, find itself transformed into a place of firebombings and tear gas, rubber bullets and live ammunition? Why, in short, did China's freest city revolt?

The Beijing government claims it's largely because of foreign (especially American, British, and Taiwanese) interference and encouragement, aided by local supporters, so-called Black Hands. Pro-Beijing groups also lament the lack of what they call "patriotic education" (what most Hong Kongers deride as Communist propaganda) and the lack of proper respect for symbols such as the flag of the People's Republic of China and the national anthem. Hong Kong, in this way of thinking, was poisoned by more than 150 years of British colonialism and needs to be more thoroughly decolonized through firm instruction by the Chinese Communist Party. This analysis is contemptuous of the Hong Kong people, as it implies that ordinary Hong Kongers don't have the ability to think for themselves. In this the Communist Party is repeating a mistake frequently made by British colonial authorities and the Hong Kong business elite; a long-standing contempt for the people of what was once one of the most remarkable cities on earth is at the core of the tragedy of Hong Kong's destruction.

The reason for the crisis is in one sense quite simple: Hong Kong people cherish their way of life and their freedoms, and they do not want to see them extinguished by a Communist regime. At its most basic level, the struggle is the age-old battle between freedom and tyranny. The 2019 protests stemmed from a hunger for freedom in a city that is being smothered by the People's Republic of China and protesters' distrust, verging on hatred, of elites in both Hong Kong and Beijing. Part of their distrust manifests itself as the sort of populist backlash that has been seen elsewhere in the world, from Brexit Britain to Orbán's regime in Hungary and Erdoğan's in Turkey. In Hong Kong's case, the anger is more pro-freedom, pro-democracy, though it does share a xenophobic (anti–mainland Chinese) taint with other populist movements. There is an understandable resentment of the vestiges of colonial white privilege that sometimes spills over into a suspicion of Western influences. Many Hong Kongers also harbor resentment toward a handful of billionaire property developers and their allies in the government who have managed to create one of the world's most unequal societies, with income disparities wider than in any other rich economy, worse even than in Zimbabwe and many other African and Latin American countries.

This resentment is exacerbated by the overwhelming numbers of mainland Chinese shoppers, mainland property buyers, and mainland workers who have come to Hong Kong in recent years. There is now a generally more "Chinese" (as in Communist Chinese) way of doing things in Hong Kong. It's summed up in the term *mainlandization*, an ugly word describing an unpleasant truth—namely, that Hong Kong is becoming more like mainland China, or the People's Republic. In 2018, there were fifty-one million mainland Chinese visitors to Hong Kong, seven for every local resident. Whole shopping areas were set up for visitors to buy everything from baby formula—the mainland had endured a series of powdered baby milk scandals that injured and even killed children—to good-quality Chinese medicine. Mainland buyers had also contributed to a boom in property prices that had seen values quintuple from the early 2000s, making apartments some of the world's most expensive, about four times as expensive as in Manhattan. Whatever the other pressures, at least Hong Kong's legal system still remained independent. In mainland China, law was used as a tool by which to rule. The sharp distinction between a Hong Kong system built on rule *of* law and a mainland one that depended on rule *by* law was one that the protesters against the extradition bill desperately wanted to preserve.

Three decades earlier, Beijing's leaders worried that the example of the then-British colony's freedoms would contaminate China. "Well water shouldn't mix with river water," contended Chinese Communist Party general secretary Jiang Zemin in warning Hong Kongers to stay out of mainland Chinese affairs. Now the situation was reversed. Swollen by three decades of high economic growth, the mainland Chinese river was rising, threatening to overrun the levees that protected Hong Kong's freedoms.

For Hong Kongers, the fight against the extradition bill wasn't about an obscure piece of legislation that would have little effect on most people. It was about a breach in the dike that would sweep away the city's freedoms. Some of my activist acquaintances, such as the *Apple Daily* newspaper founder Jimmy Lai, said it would mean the end of everything that separated Hong Kong's "well water" from the mainland "river water"—a free press, the freedom to protest, the right to a fair trial, and the other trappings of everyday life that are taken for granted in a free society. Lai's doomsday scenario seemed far-fetched to me. But these sorts of warnings struck a chord with many people in the city.

✻

The following Sunday, June 9, I went back to Victoria Park with Rena, a British friend who had also lived in Hong Kong since 1992. In my twenty-seven years in Hong Kong, I had often watched but never joined a protest march. I had come as a journalist for the *Far Eastern Economic Review* and later worked for *BusinessWeek* before stints as editor in chief at both *The Standard* and the *South China Morning Post,* Hong Kong's two English-language newspapers. As a journalist, I had met many of the key players but had avoided taking public political positions. Since 2007, I had been the executive director of the Asia Business Council, whose members were made up of corporate chiefs from countries ranging from Saudi Arabia to Indonesia to Japan. All the council's Hong Kong–based members had close ties with the government, and out of deference to my position working for them, I thought it would not be right to join protests. Somehow, though, even if Lai's warnings seemed a bit overdone, what was happening in 2019 appeared different to me, the threat more urgent after years of the mainland chipping away at the territory's freedoms.

The protest on June 9 was six or seven times larger than the one at the Tiananmen commemoration five days earlier, with an estimated one million people, one of the largest marches in Hong Kong history. This was an overwhelmingly Hong Kong Chinese crowd. Rena and I were among a handful of non-Chinese. There were children carried in backpacks and pushed in strollers; groups of students, parents, and white-haired grandparents. It was a cross section of Hong Kong, a peaceful reminder of who made up the city.

Despite predictions of a large event, the police allowed the protest march to go along only one side of Hennessy Road, one of the main streets leading from Victoria Park toward Central. Funneling one million people into a single three-lane road was a recipe for trouble. The bottled-up crowd grew impatient, but the police refused to engage in dialogue. They had been friendly and helpful in years past, but now they wouldn't meet anyone's eyes, let alone talk to people. After forty-five minutes, Rena and I had advanced about two blocks, reaching the Sogo department store. We slipped out of the throng and onto an overpass and proceeded onto a side street that paralleled Hennessy. We were in Wanchai, the mythical home of Suzie Wong and the many bars that catered mainly to Western men attracted by the Chinese and Filipina hostesses. It was another Sunday afternoon, and the men drank their beers, apparently oblivious to the historic events unfolding a block away. History was passing them by in a march that would end at the Central Government Complex, two miles from Victoria Park. The protesters' anger intensified as dusk fell, and the crowd swelled outside the government offices. Rena and I left, but it was plain that peoples' patience with the government was running out.

❧

Why did I march? I answered this question in a short piece I wrote for the pro-democracy newspaper *Apple Daily*:

> I marched because I am afraid. Afraid that the Hong Kong I love will disappear.
>
> I marched because Hong Kong needs freedom. Freedom for economic prosperity. Freedom for the rule of law.
>
> I marched because Hong Kong needs freedom from rule by law. Freedom to joke about Winnie-the-Pooh. Freedom so that people can feel safe in their homes, feel safe in their schools, feel safe in their workplaces.
>
> I marched to keep Hong Kong safe. Safe from government-sponsored kidnapping. Safe from a legal system designed to serve the state and keep the Party in power.

I marched because Hong Kong people deserve fairness and they deserve fair trials.

I marched because the Hong Kong government no longer listens to its people.

I marched because this is the year 2019, no longer a time of emperors.

I marched so that thoughts would not become crimes.

I marched because I love Hong Kong.

(The reference to Winnie-the-Pooh reflects China's censorship of the storybook bear because of his resemblance to Chinese leader Xi Jinping, an absurd example of the lengths to which China takes censorship.)

The extradition bill seemed all but certain to pass a crucial vote three days later, on June 12, at the Legislative Council's (or Legco's) regular Wednesday session. The government had accelerated the legislative timetable before opposition could intensify. That day, a crowd estimated at forty thousand people forced a postponement of the vote when they blocked legislators from entering the government complex. Police responded to the demonstrators with a savagery the city had never seen, using pepper spray, rubber bullets, and batons. New uniforms of the force's tactical squad displayed no identifying information, making individual police accountability virtually impossible. Videos of police beating protesters who had been subdued and firing tear gas indiscriminately at trapped protesters circulated widely online, stoking community anger.

Allegations of misconduct were serious enough that Amnesty International later that month issued a report on the day's events, *How Not to Police a Protest: Unlawful Use of Force by Hong Kong Police*. Nonetheless, Hong Kong's chief executive (the head of the government), Carrie Lam, backed the police chief in calling the protests a riot, thus subjecting those arrested to more serious charges. For many Hong Kongers, the police violence and Lam's refusal to question the force marked a turning point. "Asia's finest," as the police liked to be called, now were jeered on the streets. Calls started for an independent investigation into the force.[2]

On Saturday, June 15, Lam shelved the extradition bill, though she refused to withdraw it completely. Her action was too late to defuse the spreading anger that now was directed more broadly at the government and the police. The next day saw the largest demonstration in Hong Kong's history. Organizers claimed that as many as two million people attended.[3] If this figure is correct, it would mean that more than one out of every four people in the city took part. The figure is even more impressive when one considers that, unlike crowds at demonstrations in Washington, DC, which can attract people from other states, this crowd came almost entirely from the 7.5 million people living in Hong Kong. Chinese citizens were under heavy pressure not to attend. Indeed, some of the few who did were later arrested.

The protests went on. Later in June, the police headquarters across from the government headquarters was surrounded, its officers and staff trapped there for much of the night. July 1, a holiday to mark the establishment (at the time of the 1997 handover to China) of the Hong Kong Special Administrative Region, saw the Legislative Council building at the government headquarters stormed. Framed photos of unpopular political leaders were smashed; others were untouched. In the legislative chamber itself, a protester used black spray paint to painstakingly efface the words "People's Republic of China" from the city's emblem behind the speaker's rostrum. She—one of the striking features of this uprising was the number of women who had frontline protest roles—or he left the words "Hong Kong" pristine. Like many others, I felt sure that the protesters had gone too far and would lose public support. I was wrong.

As the summer wore on, the protests spread throughout the city. Marches had almost always been confined to a narrow strip of Hong Kong Island, in the historic heart of the city. In July, demonstrations moved across the harbor, to Kowloon and the New Territories, where most people live. A protest in a shopping mall saw police beating people; a photo captured a terrified woman clutching an LVMH bag as she rushed past a fallen demonstrator.[4] Thugs, acting with police collusion, or least indifference, attacked unarmed protesters on July 21 in the Yuen Long Mass Transit Railway (MTR) station, in the territory's northwest. That same night, protesters threw paint at the central government's Hong Kong and Macau Affairs Office, the body overseeing the territory. It was the first attack on a mainland office. Pro-mainland political figures began warning that red lines were being crossed.

Still, the demonstrators refused to back off. In the 1970s, martial artist Bruce Lee had shown the world a different side of Hong Kong in his films. Lee embraced the idea to "be water," a fluid, flowing, evanescent, sparkling force that was everywhere and nowhere, sometimes as elusive as mist and other times as powerful as a mountain torrent. Now Hong Kong protesters embraced Lee's "Be Water" spirit, sometimes flowing in unstoppable masses of a million or more people, sometimes pulling back in the face of police force, dispersing only to collect again. Lee wouldn't be pushed around by anyone, whether it was the Italian Mafia or Chinese gangsters. Neither would Hong Kong's millions of protesters.

❀

It is a moonlit night at the end of September 2019. I'm on the rooftop of a twenty-one-story industrial building on Hong Kong Island, thanks to a friend visiting from New York. There's red wine, prosciutto, poetry. A filmmaker among the group has just come from a demonstration in Wanchai, where the police fired a live bullet to warn the crowd, one of the first times this has happened. The government has started shutting the MTR as a way of controlling protests. While we were on our way to this gathering, our subway train passed beneath the street clashes. I had been reluctant to go out, but my friend had been eager to attend. At ten o'clock sharp, the filmmaker and others in the group begin to yell antigovernment slogans like "Liberate Hong Kong, Revolution in Our Time." From the apartment blocks that tower above us come other shouts, antigovernment slogans, part of a collective scream that takes place every night at this time, protests protected by the anonymity of the dark, people reminding themselves and one another that they are not alone.

Five days after the moonlit poetry evening, the Hong Kong government stripped away some of that anonymity, invoking emergency powers from the 1920s colonial era to outlaw face masks at demonstrations. There was talk about restricting the internet. A darker period began, one in which the Hong Kong government used a variety of legal and administrative measures to try to contain the protests. Police tactics against demonstrators, but also against medics and journalists, became harsher, the strategy being to repress the uprising, legally if possible, violently if necessary.

※

Reformist premier Zhu Rongji, who shepherded China's entry into the World Trade Organization, said that it would be China's shame if it could not run Hong Kong well. "If Hong Kong is messed up after it is returned to us, we would have betrayed the motherland," he warned. China has certainly not run Hong Kong well. The past twenty-four years have been a time of squandered opportunities. Political considerations and a desire to please a new set of colonial masters in Beijing have undermined what for the half century after World War II was one of the world's most extraordinary places, a stunning demonstration of how free people and a free economy can create economic prosperity and a unique culture of freedom from the wreckage of war and revolution. This book will try to answer questions Chinese leaders should be asking themselves: Who lost Hong Kong? How did we mess it up? It also poses questions for people in other countries, especially those neighboring China, for example: What can we learn from the Hong Kong experience about how China subverts freedom in order to better protect ourselves and our societies?

TWO

AN UMBRELLA OCCUPATION

A NEW GENERATION REBELS

"Occupy Central with Love and Peace." University of Hong Kong professor Benny Tai's 2014 plan for a midyear takeover of Central, the business district, sounded like a harmless version of Occupy Wall Street; its Woodstock overtones, of the sort rarely found in Asia, initially made it impossible for me to take the plan seriously. It seemed like just more wishful thinking from the pro-democrats.

While getting my hair cut in May of that year, I understood that the movement was for real. "I am telling all my clients that I may be shutting the shop beginning in July," my barber, Matthew, told me. As soon as Occupy Central started, Matthew intended to be there, and if it meant shutting the business for the duration, he and his family were ready. Matthew had been cutting my hair for twenty years. For the first ten years, he insisted that he didn't care about politics. It was only in 2004, when I became publisher and editor in chief of *The Standard* newspaper, that he figured I was serious about Hong Kong and could be trusted. Then it was worth his time to open up.

Matthew in most other settings likely would have prioritized stability over change. He had left school at sixteen and become a hairstylist.

In his early twenties, he'd struck out on his own, opening his own shop. His wife worked as a medical technician at Hong Kong Baptist Hospital. They had bought their flat shortly after their only child, a daughter, was born in 2002. Matthew was a devout Christian, intensely involved with his church. Matthew owned property, had his own business and a wife and daughter. One might assume he'd be a conservative, pro-government voter. Instead, he loathed the government.

Coincidentally or not, another small businessman whom I knew, a tailor named John, shared similar politics. While Matthew was reticent for a decade before expressing his views, John was bombastic, freely spewing his hatred of the Chinese Communist Party and its allies in the Hong Kong government from the first time I met him around the time of the handover. It was the millions of people like John and Matthew who had convinced another businessman, a garment manufacturer and the founder of the Giordano chain of retail clothing stores named Jimmy Lai, that his plan to start a pro-democracy newspaper just before the handover to China in the 1990s had a good chance of success.

When I talked to Matthew and John and others like them, they didn't give the government any credit for a world-class public health care system that contributed to the world's longest life expectancies. They didn't credit the government for its part in nurturing an economic boom that saw the city transformed within two generations from a place of muddy shantytowns to one of the world's wealthiest territories. They didn't give the government any points for infrastructure like the MTR subway system that set Hong Kong apart from almost any city in the world. There was no gratitude expressed for a public housing system that sheltered close to half the territory's 7.5 million people. There was no acknowledgment of the success that had been achieved in taking a colony literally overrun with more than a million refugees and making it one of the most prosperous places on earth. There was no appreciation voiced for the city's low crime rate, one that allowed women and children to go pretty much anywhere in the territory at any time of the day or night with a feeling of security.

Instead, it all came down to freedom. People in Hong Kong had personal freedom. They had civil liberties. They could go to whatever church they wanted and read whatever newspaper they wanted. But they did not have political freedom. People like Matthew didn't think about independence from China—not when they couldn't even elect their mayor or city council.

Hong Kong people have gotten used to their freedoms. The last years of British colonial rule saw the "Patten Spring," when traditional civil liberties were expanded to include political liberties as well. The first Legislative Council elections were held. The Basic Law provided for a path to universal suffrage. China and its backers in Hong Kong went further. In the run-up to the handover, and for a few years after 1997, the government, the business elites, and pro-Beijing forces repeatedly promised that universal suffrage would come in 2007, as provided for under the Basic Law. "How Hong Kong develops its democracy in the future is entirely within the autonomy of Hong Kong," Lu Ping, the director of the Hong Kong and Macau Affairs Office, told the official *People's Daily* in 1993.[1] Beijing didn't simply renege on those promises. It never showed any attempt to fulfill them. Hong Kongers had felt that in the last years of British colonial rule they at last were moving on a path to democracy, one for which their education and their experience with civic life had prepared them. Now they felt the noose tightening.

❧

The Qianlong emperor in the late eighteenth century ended his edicts with an ominous admonition: "Tremble and Obey." On August 31, 2014, the National People's Congress, China's legislative body, handed down the modern-day equivalent. The NPC decreed that any potential chief executive must "be a person who loves the country and loves Hong Kong." In mainland-speak, this meant only pro-Beijing candidates need apply. Moreover, only "two or three" candidates could run, and they would have to be screened.

Forget about Deng Xiaoping's promise of "Hong Kong people ruling Hong Kong." The cadres from Beijing would remain in charge. Hopes for Occupy Central, an event that had been pushed back from midyear to September, appeared dashed. Occupy architect Benny Tai said as much in an interview to Bloomberg published a few days after the NPC's decree, September 2.[2]

That same evening, I moderated a closed-door discussion on the current political situation in the wake of the decree with a diverse group of insiders, ranging from a former British diplomat who had been involved with the handover negotiations to a member of the Executive Council, a body that advised the chief executive and was roughly akin to the territory's cabinet. The gathering of about two dozen people included academics, journalists, and businesspeople. The attendees either occupied positions of power or met and dealt with those in power on a regular basis. They were moderate, but mostly not pro-Beijing. Although this was very much an establishment crowd, and the meeting was held at one of the bastions of colonial elite power, the Hong Kong Club, the mood was gloomy—not because of Benny Tai's admission of defeat, a climbdown that almost everyone in the room would have welcomed, but because of the August 31 National People's Congress decision to take away any hope that Hong Kong could chart a course for universal suffrage. Beijing had spoken. The door to reform was shut. Central was not to be occupied, love and peace notwithstanding.

I mention this Hong Kong Club gathering, Benny Tai's Bloomberg interview, and my earlier encounter with Matthew, to show how we all got it wrong. Perhaps only Matthew among those I spoke with—the only one who was not an insider—had it right. For, what happened at the end of the month surprised Benny Tai, surprised me, and I'm sure surprised every one of the two dozen people who had been at that Hong Kong Club meeting.

In late September, a high school student named Joshua Wong, who had emerged two years earlier as a student leader in the Scholarism movement (against mainland-influenced school textbooks), led a crowd that stormed the grounds of the Legislative Council and sparked a seventy-nine-day takeover of Central. The protesters streamed into the streets, taking over the Connaught Road / Harcourt Road highway and service road, thus shutting down a major thoroughfare spanning from the Hong Kong Club and the Mandarin Hotel to the west, to the People's Liberation Army headquarters and the Tamar government headquarters several hundred yards to the east. There were teach-ins and guitar music. Office workers went to their offices by day and sang and protested at night. Students skipped classes but worked on their homework assignments on the pavement. There was a flowering of protest art: music, posters, paintings. Where the official narrative had Hong Kong as a place of shopping malls and mindless consumerism, the truth was that its young people, far from being slackers, possessed a wealth of creative talent waiting to be unleashed. Woodstock had, after all, come to Hong Kong.

The events that led to 2014's Occupy Central, also known as the Umbrella Movement, were both improbable and the product of forces that had been building for many years. After the August 31 NPC decision that Hong Kong's political development would be indefinitely stunted, activists organized a series of events. Coincidentally, also in August 2014, I had started a Ph.D. program in history at the University of Hong Kong. I was on campus for the start of the semester's classes, Monday, September 23. This was also the day the student strike began. The campus, set on a steep hillside two miles west of Central, was crowded with students going to classes. Other than some posters, there was little sign of any student political action. I had done my undergraduate degree at the University of California, Berkeley, beginning in 1975, and on almost any given day in the late 1970s, Cal's Sproul Plaza had more political activity than what I saw at HKU on the day the strike began. The action was happening across the harbor, at the Chinese University of Hong Kong, where some thirteen thousand students from around the territory had rallied in support of the strike. It was an impressive turnout and one that boded well for the series of as-yet-undetermined events that would culminate around the time of China's National Day, October 1.[3]

I was studying for my Ph.D. even as I continued to work full time, so I spent many weekend hours in the university's main library, particularly in the Special Collections area, which houses much of the library's Hong Kong–related material. While I was reading governors' reports from the 1870s and microfilm copies of the *South China Morning Post* from the 1950s, a new chapter of history was being written two miles to the east, at the Central Government Complex.

The last Sunday in September, after a day spent under the fluorescent lights and in the chill of an over-air-conditioned concrete library building, I decided to walk home via the Peak. The university backs on to Hong Kong's Peak, an 1,800-foot-high mountain that towers over the sea-level Central District and, indeed, the entire island. (Hong Kong Island is almost one and a half times the size of Manhattan.) There is only one way to drive to the Peak, but there are three small, paved roads that allow access by foot. Hatton Road leaves from the rear entrance of the university, and I walked up it, my backpack filled with my laptop and books, and around the loop of Lugard Road, a contour road that circles the Peak at about 1,200 feet.

The view from Lugard Road is extraordinary: one looks down on the crowded skyscrapers of Hong Kong Island and across the harbor to the city of Kowloon, and to Lion Rock and the other mountains that give Kowloon its name ("Nine Dragons"). To the west, the view is of the mouth of the Pearl River Delta, with the former Portuguese colony of Macau hidden about ten miles behind Hong Kong's largest island, Lantau, the site of the territory's airport. When I first visited Hong Kong, in 1987, it struck me as a place that combined the mountains and water of the San Francisco Bay Area with the energy and dynamism of New York City—and this was the ideal spot from which to appreciate the city. Dazzling neon lights framed the harbor on a muggy September evening. The heat of the wet Hong Kong summer hadn't broken, though it was a few degrees cooler on the Peak. I wondered what was happening at the demonstration.

I walked along Lugard Road to where it ends at the Peak Tram and then down Old Peak Road, a ridiculously steep grade that was hard to descend, let alone ascend. Until the Tram was built, in 1888, Old Peak Road had been plied by sedan chair bearers carrying the governor and other rich foreigners up to the cooler climes of the Peak. The Peak Lookout, a stone building next to the Tram—it is now a popular restaurant—was once a resting place for the sedan bearers.

Back at our apartment, I read an email message from a Hong Kong friend living in London. She expressed outrage over the way that the Hong Kong government had treated the protesters. This was the first I knew that something bad had happened. Her message wasn't specific, but I soon found out that shortly before I left the library, the first of eighty-seven tear gas volleys had been fired. This was, it's believed, the first time that the Hong Kong Police had fired tear gas at their fellow citizens since the 1967 Cultural Revolution riots. (Tear gas had been used against protesters during the 2005 World Trade Organization ministerial meeting in Hong Kong, but most of those protesters were Korean farmers, so Hong Kongers generally regarded that as a different case.) In 1967, scores of people died in months of riots, many of them killed by bombs planted by Maoist radicals. But this was just another peaceful Hong Kong protest. Why had the police reacted so strongly?

I decided to see for myself what was happening. In 2014, protests were quite contained and invariably peaceful, so my plan seemed reasonable enough, the tear gas volleys notwithstanding. I walked the short distance from our apartment down to Central, less than a mile away. Except for the sound of police sirens, it seemed like another Sunday evening for most of the walk. It wasn't until I got within a few hundred yards of the mile-plus-long corridor where the streets had been occupied that anything seemed unusual.

The streets had been taken over. An expressway and service road were filled with people. There were occasional whiffs of tear gas from volleys from a hundred or more yards away, but mostly the scene was just confusing. Lines of police blocked some streets, but demonstrators otherwise moved freely throughout the downtown area, coming and going from the protest. I walked out onto Connaught Road, a six-lane road that had always been filled with fast-moving traffic. This night, it was filled with exuberant demonstrators. Occupy Central had turned this demonstration into something new, a surreal takeover of the streets.

Having lived in Korea and seen many set-piece standoffs between Seoul's riot police, who were liberal in their use of tear gas, and Molotov-throwing student protesters, I found Hong Kong's protests much more low-key. But there were rules in Korea. In Hong Kong, the rules were breaking down. The unprecedented yet ineffective use of tear gas would prove a mistake. No official inquiry was conducted into its use; it appears to have been a case of police who were inexperienced in crowd-control tactics trying to prove they were tough in the absence of an actual strategy.

What had happened? How had the pro-democracy movement gone from the defeatism expressed by Benny Tai three weeks earlier to the exuberance of students and pro-democracy allies seizing the streets? The pseudonymous Kong Tsung-gan's *Umbrella: A Political Tale from Hong Kong,* on which much of my chronology relies, tells a story of gutsy students and authorities who were both unprepared and inept.

On Friday night, a group of students led by Scholarism activist Joshua Wong simply rushed through the gate of what had formerly been an open space in front of the government headquarters: Civic Square, designed as a place where citizens could gather in a complex that was itself intended to symbolize the openness of the government to people. The site in Tamar, Hong Kong's administrative center, would be, in the words of former chief executive Donald Tsang, "an exemplification of our strong conviction that we should always be people-oriented, open-minded and receptive to public opinion."[4] Authorities had recently walled off Civic Square. In doing so, they made it more attractive as a target for protest. (I am tempted to break my general rule about engaging in counterfactual history here to wonder if, had there been no newly constructed fence, Occupy Central would have taken place.) Before the 1997 handover, the gates of the Central Government Offices on Lower Albert Road in Central had been unlocked, allowing anyone to enter or even simply pass through the complex, as I did many times.

In responding to the unrest, the government and its police piled errors on top of mistakes on top of misjudgments. Although they arrested a handful of people along with Joshua Wong on Friday night, they did not clear Civic Square until the next afternoon, after arresting sixty-one people.[5] But thousands of demonstrators remained on the streets outside the fenced-off Civic Square area, on Tim Mei Avenue. Repeated pepper spray attacks by the police on Saturday and Sunday angered demonstrators without dispersing them. The umbrellas that would become synonymous with the movement were used that weekend, perhaps for the first time and certainly more than ever before.

The occupation continued throughout that long Saturday night. At 1:40 a.m. on Sunday, September 28, Benny Tai—who had all but proclaimed the movement's defeat four weeks earlier and who had continued to postpone the announcement of when Occupy would start or how disruptive it should aim to be—proclaimed that Occupy Central had begun. Now that the students had started an occupation, Tai and the older generation had decided to join in. In making his declaration, Tai was flanked by his co-Occupy leaders (Chan Kin-man and Reverend Chu Yiu-ming) as well as longtime pro-democracy figures Jimmy Lai, Martin Lee, and Cardinal Joseph Zen.

The crowd continued to grow on Sunday. Police—who had hemmed in the demonstrators on Tim Mei Avenue, a short street on the east side of the government complex—let people leave but would not let anyone enter that area, which was isolated from the main part of the city to the south by an eight-lane road cutting it off from the Admiralty MTR station and a complex of shopping malls and office towers. The harbor was to the north, and the People's Liberation Army headquarters to the west. To the east was a nondescript no-man's-land that was also cut off by the highway. Police prohibited access to the Tim Mei Avenue protesters via the single pedestrian bridge over the eight-lane Connaught/Harcourt Road highway to the south. Increasingly large crowds gathered on the south side of that highway, unable to join up with the Tim Mei Avenue protesters because of the police cordon. As the crowd grew, the police who had kettled protesters in turn found themselves surrounded.

The crowds kept coming as evening approached. An activist I first met in 2017, whom I will call Yan, was there. When we spoke in 2021, the events of seven years earlier were vivid in his mind. He described for me the moment when the crowds first surged into Harcourt Road, and it became apparent that this wasn't just another demonstration.

We were just standing there, then both sides of the crowd went onto the motorway. We stopped the traffic on Harcourt Road. We just walked out and stopped cars. Within 15 minutes, the first tear gas was fired. A tear gas canister dropped 100 meters away from me. Nobody knew what to do. People who went on the motorway weren't the career activists, they were just ordinary people.

Author Kong Tsung-gan offers a nuanced perspective of the event, the moment when Occupy truly started:

People were trying their hardest to stay on the pavement, following that old Hong Kong impulse to obey, whether traffic rules or the police, and remain orderly. And then . . . someone stepped out into the street. [This was not a casual act. The middle six lanes are a limited-access highway, and the steady stream of traffic there moves at more than thirty-five miles an hour.] Who, what, where exactly and what it was that had motivated him, her, them, were all unclear. No one had called for people to do so. Once the first had, the crowd swelled en masse, as if a single organism had been given a mysterious push, heaving out into the streets. Cars, taxis, buses, mini-buses slowed, stopped. The traffic ceased. There would be no further traffic on that stretch of Connaught/Harcourt until mid-December, 75 days into the future.[6]

By a little after 7 p.m., shortly after I had left the library and was walking up Hatton Road to the Peak, the police had fired a total of nineteen tear gas canisters. By the time I returned home at around 8 p.m., the total had risen to twenty-one. By the end of the night, the police reported that they had fired eighty-seven rounds of tear gas.[7]

As my friend's message to me from London foreshadowed, the tear gas quickly stoked outrage around the world. It increased demonstrators' anger and seemingly made them more determined. The sight of umbrellas being raised as protection against the gas symbolized the nonviolent pro-democracy protesters standing up to a Communist state.

In the weeks that followed, the government and demonstrators settled into a standoff. The demonstrators continued to press for universal suffrage. The government refused to negotiate. One inconclusive debate took place between three student leaders and Carrie Lam, then the secretary for administration. But the government just waited the demonstrators out. There were enough citizens in Hong Kong who were afraid of Beijing or who simply wanted order and stability and a return to normalcy that support for the demonstrators waned.

At the University of Hong Kong, classes and life went on more or less as usual while the occupation rumbled on just two miles away. The inside of the student center, visible behind glass windows I passed on my way from the history department to the main library, along the campus's pedestrian University Walk, was piled high with bottles of water and snacks that would be distributed to protesters. In mid-October, I took a picture of two pieces of paper that had been taped to the imitation redbrick wall along the new walk. In large, computer-printed letters, a sign asked, "If Not Now, Then When?" Below, someone had handwritten in blue marker, "If Not Us, Then Who?" A foot away, among the jumble of posters on the wall, one advertised a lecture organized by the General Education Unit of the University of Hong Kong, entitled, "Will China Stocks Flood the Hong Kong Market?" It explained: "This lecture will talk about Hong Kong's prospects as a major listing centre for mainland companies and the recent development of listings from China."

I'm sure I wasn't the only one who noted the irony of promoting China's increased presence in Hong Kong even as students were protesting against this same encroachment. On the same wall, an informational TV screen that typically advertised campus events played loops of protest videos. HKU students were at the center of the Occupy Central movement, and the fight for democracy was visible everywhere, and yet other, more common activities continued. It was a very Hong Kong jumble, a mash-up of often contradictory elements in close proximity—the arrival of mainland stocks to dominate the Hong Kong bourse was both a promise and a threat.

Indeed, one of the common complaints from Hong Kong residents, even those who sympathized with the pro-democracy movement, concerned the way that international media coverage unfairly framed Hong Kong. The BBC, CNN, and other Western media in particular, showed images of Hong Kong that suggested a city consumed by protests. This is the nature of media, and I could never really understand the complaints. Would they be more likely to watch reports of daily life in, say, Beirut—or would they watch a bombing? Would viewers watch people drinking coffee at Parisian cafés—or Notre Dame in flames? The events of 2014 were dramatic, but they also took place in the context of a city of over seven million people who mostly went about their daily business without undue inconvenience. Other than disrupting traffic—and most Hong Kongers didn't own cars—the demonstration did not have a big impact.

*

But Occupy woke up many people. One of those was Edward Chin, a middle-aged Hong Kong Canadian finance industry professional. I first met Chin on the street in 2017 when he was campaigning for a district council seat to represent the elite Peak district. I stopped to talk to him at the corner of MacDonnell Road and Garden Road in Mid-Levels, an affluent residential area, where he stood waving at motorists and talking to the occasional passerby. By chance, I met him again at the pan-democratic primary in July 2020, and we later talked about his experience. He typified the reasonable, middle- to upper-middle-class sorts of professionals who supported the democracy movement.

Chin had grown up in a middle-class Hong Kong family and had attended the elite Diocesan Boys' School. (Benny Tai was four years his senior at the school.) Born in 1968, Chin left for high school in Minnesota in 1984, at age sixteen, part of the first wave of children being sent abroad by parents anxious about the prospect of Chinese rule. He attended the University of Minnesota before his parents immigrated to Canada. He joined them there and graduated from the University of Manitoba before earning an MBA at the University of Toronto. The Tiananmen killings of 1989 radicalized him, and he organized a lecture by the prominent dissident Wu'er Kaixi in Toronto. But life and work intervened, and Chin started a successful career in finance, first in Canada and, after 2000, in Hong Kong. The first demonstration that he attended was the July 1, 2003, rally against Article 23, a watershed demonstration in Hong Kong history and one that attracted an estimated five hundred thousand people.

Benny Tai's January 2013 article in the newspaper the *Hong Kong Economic Journal* called for a campaign of civil disobedience—this was the original articulation of the "Occupy Central with Love and Peace" movement. The article prompted Chin—who had written a column for the same paper since 2006—to reach out to his old schoolmate; while at Diocesan, the two had both been in Goodban House—Tai, four years older, had been the house prefect—and their tie proved enduring. They met up at the upscale Landmark shopping mall in Central for coffee and ended up talking for ninety minutes about why Tai had written the article and the importance of civil disobedience in winning universal suffrage.

Chin went away from their meeting believing that "we must do something more than the normal July 1 rally," so he formed a group of finance professionals to push for democracy. "Finance people usually say we should focus on money and not be political. Hong Kong is not just about extracting as much profit as possible. If there is no fair play, that is not Hong Kong. There are a lot of other things that make up Hong Kong, like freedom and the rule of law," he later told me.

These sorts of sentiments saw Chin's column canceled at the end of August 2014, shortly before Occupy Central started. The paper told him the column would be cut because of a page redesign, a laughable claim to Chin, who told an interviewer at the time that it was all about politics. "About six months ago, I was told to write less about politics," he said. "Because of the political and economic situation in today's Hong Kong, there's no way for me to write only about finance in my column, since politics and economics are fundamentally inseparable."[8] The *Hong Kong Economic Journal*, long known for its independence, had been bought in 2006 by Richard Li, son of billionaire Li Ka-shing, one of Asia's wealthiest men. Tycoon ownership of newspapers in Hong Kong and throughout Asia made it more difficult for the press to function as an independent watchdog.

At the end of 2013, Chin, along with a group of other finance industry professionals, founded the Banking and Finance Professionals in Support of Occupy Central. In the spring of 2014, the group bought space in major newspapers, including *The New York Times*, *The Wall Street Journal*, the *Financial Times*, and, in Hong Kong, the

Apple Daily, to publish almost absurdly reasonable open letters, published as advertisements, to President Xi Jinping that read like a humble petition to the emperor. Titled, "Ten Requests to the Communist Party of China from the People of Hong Kong (Finance and Banking Sector)," their petition, addressed also to Zhang Xiaoming (director of the Liaison Office of the Central People's Government in Hong Kong), began with an expression of loyalty on the part of the signatories as citizens and believers in the goodwill and good intentions of the central government: "We are all Hong Kong permanent residents who truly love the country and Hong Kong. We wholeheartedly believe that the central government of China is one that serves and seeks the greatest wellbeing for the people of Hong Kong." The statement makes an appeal to the traditional Chinese notion of harmony in its plea for the government to listen to its people.

> Since Hong Kong's reversion to the motherland, the Hong Kong Government policies have increasingly fallen short of applying the principle of "one country, two systems" and the policy objectives of the Basic Law. This has created a perception that the Hong Kong Government has not been listening to the voice of Hong Kong people, creating deep-seated conflicts across various spectrums in our society. The current political climate in Hong Kong is having a negative impact to [*sic*] Hong Kong's competitiveness as a major financial centre in Asia. Hong Kong's existing political system has become the stumbling block to the city's long-term social, political and economic growth, and is the root cause of social division and disharmony in Hong Kong.

The ten-point petition covers terrain that had been traversed repeatedly over the past two decades. It asks for universal suffrage; that the rule of law be safeguarded; that freedom of press, speech, assembly, and worship be upheld; and that the Hong Kong government be empowered to independently adopt policies in areas such as immigration in order to facilitate the flow of professional talent for the finance sector. There were calls to strengthen anticorruption mechanisms. Only on the final point did the group go beyond mainstream Hong Kong sentiment, saying out loud what most people would not have dared: calling for democracy in Hong Kong as a test run for democracy in China ("Create and facilitate universal suffrage for Hong Kong which can be leveraged as a blueprint for democratic elections in China to advance China's progress toward democracy").

The open letter was published two years into Xi's rule. There was hope at the time that he might be a reformer. Few people imagined that he would become the most powerful and autocratic leader since Mao Zedong. Although it's been less than a decade since the petition was published, the call for Hong Kong to provide "a blueprint" for democracy in China now seems audacious, even reckless.

Chin is a middle-class professional, occasional newspaper columnist, and the spokesperson for a tiny group that claims no more than 150 members. Yet he causes enough trouble in the eyes of authorities to invite harassment. At the beginning of 2019, he organized a small demonstration protesting the arrest of Michael Kovrig and Michael Spavor, two Canadians detained by China in retaliation for Canada's detention of Huawei executive Meng Wanzhou. After the demonstration in support of the two Michaels, authorities came to his house eight times over the following twenty-four hours to interrogate him.

When we spoke in early 2021, shortly after fifty-five people were arrested for their part in the July 2020 pan-democratic primary (which we'll discuss later in this book), Chin's tone remained moderate even as he wondered if he might be swept up in a rumored new wave of arrests. "What I am most concerned about is whether we still have autonomy, one country, two systems, as promised in the Basic Law and the [Sino-British] Joint Declaration." If Chin sounds reasonable, that's because he is. If anything, before the start of Occupy Central, the demonstrators were often faulted for being too reasonable for too long.

Nevertheless, it was in 2014 that China's paranoia over Hong Kong independence developed. Beijing and its allies have focused on what they say are secessionist activities in Hong Kong. The issue of independence has touched a particularly raw nerve and has been used to justify the harsh National Security Law introduced in 2020. Ironically, the pro-independence movement was stoked, if not largely created, by Chief Executive C. Y. Leung during his five years in office from 2012 to 2017.

Beginning around 2013, pro-Beijing political figures began complaining about the use of colonial flags. "The Chinese people will not accept some Hongkongers waving the colonial flag," Chinese Politburo standing committee member Yu Zhengsheng was quoted as saying. Another official complained that "the decolonization process—Hongkongers shaking off their mentality as colonial subjects—has not yet been completed."[9]

The flags were seen as evidence of an incipient pro-independence movement. In the summer of 2014, I was in Central, observing the July 1 march coming from Victoria Park to the east. At the heart of Central, where Chater Road breaks off from Des Voeux Road, the march doubled back to the east, toward government headquarters. It was there that I saw the notorious colonial flag that had earlier attracted criticism. There was a single marcher holding it, perhaps with two or three friends. There were no signs about independence, no chanting of slogans, and no evidence of any sort of organized network. In fact, it wasn't even clear what the point of the flag was. Nostalgia? Protest? Who knew? I had never heard anyone talk about independence in Hong Kong. Anyway, how did an outdated colonial flag come to signify an independence movement?

Leung, who had long-standing pro-Beijing connections but has denied reports that he is a Communist Party member, seemed to see conspiracies everywhere. He attacked the three editors of a student magazine for allegedly espousing pro-independence views. One of them was among a small number of undergraduates in a history seminar I took at the University of Hong Kong the following spring. He was a quiet and serious senior, who said almost nothing during the graduate-level course. I was stunned when I learned that he was one of the editors of this purported independence magazine. Scholars will try to figure this out someday, but it seems to me that Leung himself created the movement. Within two years of that 2014 article, something like one out of five Hong Kongers supported independence.

Was this a deliberate trap that Leung had wanted to set? Or did he unwittingly create the very thing he most feared? I later asked my activist friend Yan about this puzzle. Here is how he summed it up:

> C. Y. Leung started the Hong Kong independence movement. Nobody talked about localism, nobody talked about independence. It is OK for young people to have crazy ideas, but independence was not in popular discourse and there was no analytical frame-work—he drummed up the issue. It was not mainstream until C. Y. Leung talked about it. If he thought he was playing some political games against some elite class person, he overplayed his hand.
>
> Once you go down the independence route, it becomes an impossible dream. Defending the Basic Law or the constitution? There is something there. But if we talk about independence, it is set up to fail. As a political agenda, I feel sorry for people who strongly believe that's the only route for Hong Kong, because it is such an impossible task.

For a long time, it was a riddle to me how the Hong Kong elite could claim that Hong Kongers didn't care about politics. After 2003, when some five hundred thousand people marched against proposed national security legislation, that myth became impossible to peddle. So, the blame shifted to abroad: the Hong Kong and Chinese establishment believe that foreign forces were behind the political upheaval. As I listened to the self-styled aristocracy more closely, it became apparent that they did not understand the Hong Kong people. They thought ordinary people were too uneducated or too stupid to organize mass movements that would shake the nation or, indeed, the world. Ignorance and arrogance blinded the elite. This made them susceptible to believe the Communist claim that hidden forces, mostly foreigners out to hurt China, were manipulating the protesters.

It had taken ten years of haircuts before Matthew confided not only that he was interested in politics but that he was politically involved. When Joshua Wong led his Scholarism movement against pro-Communist textbooks, Matthew was among the fifty thousand people who joined them after work in demonstrating at government headquarters. Around Hong Kong there were millions of people like Matthew. They were schooled in subservience and obsequiousness, taught to regurgitate the correct answers on exams and to keep their mouths shut, to be seen and not heard. It was a shock to the ruling class when they refused to shut up and instead spoke out.

※

After seventy-nine days, Occupy Central ended in late 2014. The government appeared to have secured a victory. No concessions were made to the protesters, yet no one was killed. Many were arrested, some were jailed, but the underlying issues remained unresolved. People wanted China to come through on the promise of universal suffrage.

A little more than two years later, at an Easter lunch in 2017, I met the activist, as mentioned earlier, whom I call Yan. In his forties, he was a Hong Kong Chinese married to a friend of a friend. I met Yan at a party, and we talked a long time about what had happened in Hong Kong. I told him how impressed I was that the Hong Kong protesters were so peaceful. He politely made it clear that he was contemptuous of this peacefulness that I found so attractive. This sort of "bourgeois" approach—I remember the irony of his using Marxist terminology to talk about his anticommunist struggle—needed to be done away with, Yan said. Rougher, more militant tactics were going to be needed. Yan's approach caught me off guard. Attitudes among a younger generation were hardening. In the absence of any movement on the government's side, patience was waning for the traditional approach of working within the legal and legislative system.

This is where the government and the party are most disingenuous. They force a consensus and use naked power to bulldoze. They don't subject their performance or their policies to anything like real public scrutiny. They know that legitimacy is important, so they manufacture fake legitimacy. Meanwhile, the 60 percent or more of Hong Kong people—the four million or so Matthews, Johns, and Yans—who support pro-democracy candidates go on cutting hair and making suits and waiting for better days to come.

In late November, a few days before Occupy was about to end, when everyone knew that the tents would soon be folded up, I went down early in the morning to walk through the site. It was a clear day, perfect for photos. I took pictures of signs and tents as the sun rose over the encampment. I was standing next to a wall of a sort that is quite common in Hong Kong: it is made of local granite, the rock that makes up the hard bedrock that anchors the city's skyscrapers. The morning light brought out the texture of this lovely rock. I took a picture. Then it hit me: this was a wall around the People's Liberation Army's downtown compound. The protesters had been literally on the edge of a PLA base for what in the end would amount to a seventy-nine-day occupation, yet no one had been killed or seriously injured. The troops had stayed in their barracks. There had been no new Tiananmen Square. Central had, after all, been occupied with love and peace.

But would the troops continue to stay in their barracks? The movement had been largely nonviolent, but could this continue in the face of the Beijing and Hong Kong governments' refusal to engage in any sort of negotiation? China had promised democracy in 2007, the Basic Law granting it a minimum of a decade after the handover in order to cement its authority and legitimacy before having to contest for power in the territory's municipal elections. The refusal of Chief Executive C.Y. Leung and Chief Secretary Carrie Lam to engage in any sort of negotiation with the Occupy Central demonstrators did not bode well.

The month after Occupy Central ended, in January 2015, media entrepreneur and pro-democracy advocate Jimmy Lai hosted a lunch at his house in the exclusive Kadoorie Avenue section of Hong Kong. Lai had sneaked into Hong Kong from the mainland at the age of twelve and made his first fortune in textiles and his second in retail, before starting pro-democracy newspapers and magazines in Hong Kong and Taiwan. It was a sunny winter day, and we ate outside, in Lai's elegant garden. But the sparkling weather and good food couldn't mask the gloomy atmosphere. Lai and others at the small lunch were disappointed that they had staged such a large-scale, long-lasting protest and yet had no political reforms to show for it. I disagreed.

Occupy Central was a historic moment when Hong Kong people nonviolently showed their determination to fight for the freedom that was guaranteed under the Basic Law. I said, and I still believe, that the Umbrella Movement will be seen much as the May 4, 1919, protests in China were. What started as a protest against the government's acceptance of the humiliating terms of the Versailles peace process after World War I became a larger assault on traditional Chinese culture. The May Fourth Movement embraced democracy and science and marks the starting point for modern China. Long after the Chinese Communist Party is consigned to the dustbin of history, people will remember the hundreds of thousands of Hong Kongers who held their umbrellas against the tear gas and spoke truth to power during a seventy-nine-day occupation of their city's core.

THREE

AND THEN THERE WERE NONE

Five publishers and booksellers disappeared one by one, so quietly that few people noticed at first. Gui Minhai was picked up at a beach resort in Thailand. Two were picked up at their wives' homes across the border in Shenzhen, in mainland China. One simply vanished. There were suspicions that mainland agents were behind the abductions, but no one knew for sure. Then, the kidnapping in Hong Kong of the fifth and final abductee, Paul Lee, at the end of 2015, left no doubt that Chinese security agents were systematically picking up the owners of the Mighty Current publishing house and its Causeway Bay Books store. Lee had gone to deliver books to someone posing as a new customer for Mighty Current's gossipy books on China's leaders. He had been pushed into a minivan and taken across the border to the mainland. And then there were none.

Hong Kong's pro-democracy community was spooked. This was the nightmare post-handover scenario, one where people exercising their civil liberties within Hong Kong were snatched. The case of the disappearing booksellers and related incidents since 1997 pointed to a systematic attempt to undermine Hong Kong's freedoms that stretches back further than the protests in 2014 and 2019. The Communist Party, it was now clear, had never been willing to tolerate a free Hong Kong.

The cover-up unraveled when one of those detained, Lam Wing-kee, was allowed by mainland authorities to return to Hong Kong with the promise that he would retrieve information useful to security operatives. Instead, Lam held a press conference where he detailed the imprisonment and forced confession he had endured in China. Even after Lam's explosive remarks, the Hong Kong government said little and, to all appearances, did less. It was apparent that the territory's timid officials would not even try to protect Hong Kong citizens from the sovereign power.

The booksellers' arrests were part of a suppression of Hong Kong's intellectual life following the end of 2014's Occupy Central. Early in 2015, cinemas abruptly stopped showings of the surprise hit movie *Ten Years*, a dystopian look at Hong Kong in 2025. The movie featured five short films made by five different directors, united only by a bleak vision of Hong Kong ten years hence. In one episode, the Communist Party stages a political assassination to push through a national security law. In another, a taxi driver loses his livelihood, and his daughter, because he cannot master Mandarin. Another features local farmers subjected to harassment and, eventually, attacks of the sort inflicted during Mao's Cultural Revolution of the 1960s.

Produced on a budget of just $64,000 (currency is in U.S. dollar amounts throughout, unless HK$ is specified), *Ten Years* pulled in more viewers than the latest *Star Wars* release at the Broadway Cinematheque, the city's premier film showcase. Then it quickly disappeared from cinemas, one of the film's directors, Zune Kwok, later told me, because no major cinema dared show it any longer. The movie won critical acclaim, with the *South China Morning Post* calling it "one of the most thought-provoking local films in years." It was nominated for Best Film at the Hong Kong Film Festival.

The movie predictably angered Chinese Communist authorities, who banned positive mentions of it on the mainland. Mainland newspaper *Global Times*, a mouthpiece for Chinese Communist chauvinism, called the film "absurd" and a "thought virus." Hong Kongers responded to having the movie shut out of cinemas by organizing community screenings. In April 2016, just before the Hong Kong Film Festival, *Ten Years* was shown at thirty-four different locations around Hong Kong in a community project that sponsored showings under highway overpasses, on the steps of the Sha Tin Town Hall, and next to the headquarters of the Legislative Council. After *Ten Years* won the Hong Kong Film Festival nomination, state-owned China Central Television (CCTV) decided not to broadcast the festival's ceremonies live for the first time since 1991.

Ten Years did win the Best Film award in 2016, prompting an angry outburst from Peter Lam, chairman of the Hong Kong Tourism Board: "The fact that the film got the prize is a tragedy for Hong Kong's movie industry [because] politics has kidnapped the profession and politicized film-awarding events." Lam is a billionaire Hong Kong property developer, better known as an avid racehorse owner than a cultural critic. It somehow passes as normal in Hong Kong that billionaires chair bodies like the Tourism Board and opine on the political correctness of movies. (Kiwi Chow, who edited the self-immolation segment, had the satisfaction of seeing his documentary of the 2019 protests, *Revolution of Our Times*, shown in a surprise screening at the 2021 Cannes Festival.)

Censorship in Chinese Hong Kong reflected a system developed during Britain's century and a half of colonialism. The colonial Special Branch was an intelligence unit attached to the police that monitored political activities. Originally set up in the 1930s, it accelerated operations after the 1967 Cultural Revolution–inspired protests and bombings. Scores of activists were held indefinitely in the late 1960s, many of them at the Victoria Road Detention Centre, which is now, ironically, a beacon of academic freedom as the site of the University of Chicago's Hong Kong campus. Special Branch spied on fledgling political movements in the 1970s and '80s. Film censorship in Hong Kong began as early as 1919. Films in the 1930s couldn't be overly critical of the Japanese. During the post-1949 period, filmmakers needed to steer clear of the rivalry between Chinese Nationalists and Communists. Hong Kong has always been political, but its political expressions have always been tightly circumscribed.

Long before the booksellers were abducted, there had been signs that China was criminalizing free thought. The jailing in 2005 of Hong Kong–born journalist Ching Cheong, a pro-Beijing media heavyweight, was a harbinger of worse to come. At the time of the 1989 Tiananmen Square Massacre, Ching was a senior executive at the pro-Beijing *Wen Wei Po* newspaper. He resigned, along with dozens of others from the newspaper, after the killings. He later joined the Singapore-based *Straits Times,* where he reported on China and Taiwan. His writings had a strong pro-China slant, favoring unification with Taiwan. Yet, for all his ties to China's Communist Party, he was arrested in 2005, convicted of spying for Taiwan, and jailed. Ching's conviction seems to relate to his writings about former Chinese premier Zhao Ziyang, who was ousted as part of the leadership coup just before the Tiananmen killings, placed under house arrest, and never seen in public again. Ching's case attracted international attention. The Hong Kong Journalists Association and the Committee to Protect Journalists collected thirteen thousand signatures on a petition to Chinese general secretary Hu Jintao asking for Ching's release. Even Hong Kong's pro-Beijing legislators called for authorities to provide evidence of Ching's guilt or release him. Ching's arrest was chilling precisely because he was seen as a Beijing loyalist. After his eventual release in 2008, the case was largely forgotten—dismissed by most people as an unfortunate aberration.

❀

As the freest city in China, Hong Kong had long been a beacon of hope in a bleak landscape. The city was home to a lively semi-underground publishing world that specialized in books on China. This business was legal, but it was not encouraged. One of its prominent members was a man named Jin Zhong. Jin was born on the mainland. His father had been a senior official in the Kuomintang (KMT), or Nationalist, government and had fled to Taiwan in 1949. Jin Zhong, his mother, and four siblings were left in the central province of Hunan. Separated first by war and then by revolution, the children never saw their father again; their mother never saw her husband again. After Jin Zhong's father died in 1978, shortly after

China's Cultural Revolution ended, the mother and one sibling were given permission to leave China to settle his estate. Other siblings followed, and in 1980 Jin Zhong arrived in Hong Kong.

Jin had been a civil engineer in China. It was not a career he had chosen—he had been assigned the profession because he was good at math. His mainland China qualifications were not valid in Hong Kong, but he didn't much care. He had always been interested in politics and current affairs—his family life had been shaped by them—and he started writing articles for local magazines in Hong Kong before working at one of the most renowned, *Seventies*. In 1987, he struck out on his own, founding a magazine initially called *Emancipation* and later retitled *Open Monthly*. "In China, there was no freedom of speech, no freedom of the press," he told me from Brooklyn, where he lives with his wife, Stacy Mosher, a translator. Stacy interpreted our conversation. I spoke in English, Stacy asked Jin questions in Cantonese, and Jin answered in his heavily accented Cantonese. We talked at the end of August 2020, two months after the National Security Law was put into place.

"When I came to Hong Kong and found freedoms, I really wanted to enjoy those freedoms," said Jin. "I became a journalist because these are precious freedoms." This notion of enjoying, protecting, and extending these sorts of "precious freedoms" drove Jin's professional life, just as it drives the lives of so many Hong Kongers.

Jin made it his calling to expose China's mistakes. "There was no freedom at all in China, in particular to criticize Mao and the Communist Party. My mission in every article I wrote and in every issue of the magazine was to point out all the wrongs that had been done by Mao and the Communist Party. That was a freedom I never would have had in China." The magazine thrived, and Jin set up a publishing house. He became what the media called a "banned books publisher," specializing in books that could not be sold in mainland China. Among its forty books were Jung Chang's *Wild Swans* and her Chinese-language edition of a Mao biography and a volume based on secret conversations with ousted premier Zhao Ziyang.

After the handover in 1997, dissident publishers like Jin played a delicate game with security agents. Visitors from the State Security

Bureau (stationed in mainland China) would let Jin know that they were coming and ask him to join them for a dinner. Although it was an offer he could not refuse, it was always put very cordially. There was never any coercion. The point seemed mostly to let Jin know that he was being watched.

"Every time I saw them, they were a little fatter," remembers Mosher, who often accompanied her husband, "because they had so many people to take out to dinner. They were perfectly pleasant. Always very nice and very courteous. You never got the feeling they were going to shoot you." They gave gifts—often food, but one time a cute pink camera for Jin's and Stacy's daughter. This was the soft side of China's surveillance-and-control tactics. They were watching, and you knew they were watching. Sometimes the meetings were with security people, but often they were with people representing organizations that were allied with the Chinese government, known as the United Front Work Department. The United Front is made up of nongovernmental organizations that follow government instructions and are an important part of China's power projection.

> This kind of United Front practice was very common and wide-spread, applied to any influential journalist, any democratic politicians—to a certain extent, anyone who had influence. There were friendly visits, I was invited to dinner, given gifts. The idea wasn't to make you do or not do something but to break down your feeling of antagonism or resistance to see that these people were people you could talk to. What happened to the Causeway Bay booksellers—those were the hard methods. For most people in Hong Kong, it was soft treatment. Their attitude was "We know what it's like. We know what others in the government are doing and, yes, they're assholes, but you can talk to us."

Tactics toughened when Jin prepared to publish a book by Yu Jie, a Chinese American democracy activist, on Xi Jinping. The dinner, held in a private room in a restaurant on Hong Kong Island, was friendly. "They made it clear that this book was different," Jin remembers. He was told that he should not under any circumstances publish it. "It was clear that these instructions had come from a high level. If I insisted on going ahead with the book, they would have sabotaged it anyway." How could they do that? I asked. "They have agents inside the printing press and mess up your publishing, cause headaches and massive delays," Jin continued. "It is not only the publisher but printers, distributors—who are all under pressure. There are printers and distributors who will not handle this sort of work. The number who will is shrinking on a daily basis. I was leaving anyway, finally moving to the U.S. to join my family, and I didn't need the headache."

It is worth underscoring Jin's assertion that the party had operatives inside printing houses and among book distributors. Some years earlier, it had emerged that almost all bookstores in Hong Kong were secretly owned by mainland interests. This insidious infiltration of the book publishing business mirrors the secretive party tactics employed throughout Hong Kong.

Jin continued:

Freedom in Hong Kong has been steadily shrinking since 1997. The shrinkage has been extreme in the last couple of years. At the time I left Hong Kong, in 2016, I still felt I could write whatever I wanted to and say whatever I wanted to. That's not the case now. The more recent changes have come about because the Chinese government became absolutely terrified by the power of the Occupy Central movement and the protests against the [extradition] legislation. Before then, the Chinese government would kind of let things slide a bit. But because those movements were so successful and so overwhelming, it made them clamp down on Hong Kong even more. The security law that was passed this year shows that the Chinese government is no longer willing to allow any more freedom in Hong Kong than in China.

It was not only dissidents who were being targeted. In early 2017, one of China's then-richest men, Xiao Jianhua, was kidnapped from the Four Seasons Hotel in Hong Kong. The *South China Morning Post* reported that five men had entered Xiao's twenty-eighth-floor suite just after 1 a.m. and left two hours later with the billionaire. Video footage shows him being wheeled out of the hotel in the middle of the night with a blanket over his head, the bevy of female bodyguards who protected him nowhere to be seen. Xiao (or someone acting on his behalf), who boasted of his connections to Chinese leaders and whose fortune peaked at an estimated $6 billion, later placed an advertisement in a Hong Kong newspaper denying that he had been abducted and asserting that he was "recuperating abroad." He has not been heard from since, his status as a naturalized Canadian offering no protection against his arbitrary detention.[1]

The abduction of the Causeway Bay booksellers in Hong Kong and in Thailand, and their arrests in China, point to a larger pattern. Even before the imposition of the vague and wide-ranging National Security Law in mid-2020, mainland China's security activities in Hong Kong had eroded the city's status as a protected enclave.

British-based human rights activist Benedict Rogers found this out firsthand when he tried to enter Hong Kong in October 2017. He had planned a discreet, low-key trip, letting only a few people know he was coming. "Somehow the news of my visit leaked to Beijing," he told me when we spoke in early 2021. "I suspect it was through intercepting emails or other forms of communications." A British MP who had contact with the Chinese embassy in London told Rogers that the embassy had called to say that they had found out he was going to Hong Kong "and asked him to tell me that I absolutely should not go and that it was outrageous I was going. They had heard that I had plans to visit Joshua Wong or Nathan Law in prison." Rogers promised that he would not visit political prisoners or give public talks or media interviews. "It would be very private and very low-key, no threat." (The fact that Rogers felt compelled to make a promise of this sort shows how much Hong Kong's freedoms had already deteriorated.)

Still, the Chinese insisted that Rogers shouldn't go and warned that he might be denied entry upon arrival. Rogers consulted with a number of key people in Hong Kong and the United Kingdom.

All of them without exception said, "We think the Chinese are bluffing. They are trying to threaten you into not getting on the plane. We think that Hong Kong's autonomy is strong enough that the decision will be in the hands of Hong Kong immigration, so don't be scared by the embassy's bullying tactics. If, in the unlikely event the Chinese are serious and will interfere, the world needs to know that. It would be a serious breach of the Basic Law and the Sino-British Declaration, and the world needs to know. The only way to find out is to try."

When Rogers reached the immigration counter in Hong Kong, the officer entered his name into her computer. When his personal details appeared on the screen, "I could see her demeanor completely change, and she looked quite scared." Her supervisor was called. "They crouched over the screen, and then the supervisor said, 'Could you come with me?'" In an interview office, a group of immigration officers questioned Rogers. Then they told him, "We're very sorry. We are under instructions not to permit you entry into Hong Kong." Within minutes, a squad of immigration officers took him in a dedicated minibus across the tarmac and put him on a plane back to Bangkok, his previous stop.

The last moment was quite moving. All of the Hong Kong immigration officers had been perfectly polite and civil—there was no hint of mistreatment. I had the impression from their body language that they really didn't want to do this, but they had clear instructions from Beijing. . . . I said to the one remaining immigration officer. 'Does the fact that you are denying me entry to Hong Kong mean One Country, Two Systems is dead?' He looked at me with some emotion. "I cannot comment on that. I am just doing my job." I replied: "I feel that this is a sad day in terms of what it represents. He looked at me and said, 'Yes, it is a sad day.'"

Hong Kong was supposed to be different from mainland China. That difference is narrowing by the day. The National Security Law imposed on Hong Kong in mid-2020, with wide-ranging definitions of sedition, subversion, terrorism, and collusion with foreign powers, makes anyone anywhere in the world subject to its provisions.

Yet China hadn't bothered to wait for the legislation before snatching people abroad. The 2015 abduction of Gui Minhai, a Swedish citizen, from his home in Thailand and his unexplained reappearance in China, where he recanted his Swedish citizenship and was sentenced to ten years' imprisonment, is an example of China's long reach.

Gui, a naturalized Swedish citizen, has been held in China for more than six years. Sweden's attempts to intercede on his behalf have resulted in bullying by the Chinese government. The Chinese ambassador to Sweden, Gui Congyou (presumably no relation to Gui Minhai), told Swedish television that reporting by the country's journalists had interfered in China's internal affairs. "It's like a forty-eight-kilogram lightweight boxer who provokes a feud with an eighty-six-kilogram heavyweight boxer, who out of kindness and goodwill urges the (smaller) boxer to take care of himself," Gui said, in comparing China's self-styled restrained behavior to a heavyweight boxer who has to deal with a featherweight. China advised Sweden "to leave and mind his own business, but the latter refuses to listen, and even breaks into the home of the heavyweight boxer. What choice do you expect the heavyweight boxer to have?"[2]

The ambassador contended, "Some Swedish media and journalists always make groundless accusations and attacks on China, instigating confrontation, hatred, and division between the two countries and peoples," and he accused Swedish journalists of "trying to think of ways to slander China." Gui said China was right to deny visas to journalists who did not want to "promote friendship, communication, understanding, and cooperation." He also threatened "counter measures" if the Swedish culture minister attended a prize ceremony honoring Gui Minhai. She did attend the ceremony, and Sweden has largely stood up to China. But not every country has the wealth or the confidence in its democratic traditions to do so.

Think about the implications of Ambassador Gui's statements. He accused journalists in Sweden, a free and democratic country, who were reporting on a case of wrongful imprisonment of a Swedish citizen (or a former citizen who may have renounced his citizenship under pressure), of acting like burglars. The ambassador remained in his post and continued to make provocative remarks. The Swedish government rejected calls for his expulsion on the grounds that the next ambassador would be no better. This is China's wolf-warrior diplomacy. It is the behavior of an aggressive nation, not one content to play by established rules.

The treatment of Gui Minhai and, indeed, Sweden shows what China intends for countries around the world when it has the strength to impose its will. China will declare no-go areas. Political leaders are already threatened with the loss of the China market and other sanctions if they meet with the Dalai Lama or Taiwan's president. An expanding and assertive China will try to define the boundaries of whom leaders can meet, what journalists can report, what politicians can discuss.

China's retaliatory behavior predated Xi Jinping's rise to power. In 2010, the Nobel Prize Committee awarded the Nobel Peace Prize to jailed Chinese dissident Liu Xiaobo. Although the committee is independent—though it is appointed by Norway's parliament—the award to Liu prompted swift Chinese action. Talks on a free trade agreement halted. China crimped imports of Norwegian salmon, claiming it was "unhealthy." Norway's share of China's imported salmon market fell from 92 percent in 2010 to 29 percent in 2013. The Norwegian winner of the 2009 Eurovision pop concert saw his trip to China canceled. Relations between the two countries were frozen for six years. Visas for Norwegian academics and businesspeople were denied for no apparent reason. Despite extolling human rights while she was in the opposition—she promised "fireworks"—Norwegian Prime Minister Erna Solberg did not bring up the issue of Liu Xiaobo during a visit to China in April 2016. Her timid approach led Chinese dissident Hu Jia to deride Solberg as a "salmon-seller."

Similar examples have proliferated in recent years. Banana shipments from the Philippines were blocked following a dispute over territory in the South China Sea; Lithuania was snubbed after a meeting with the Dalai Lama. Australian shipments of products ranging from barley to wine to beef were curtailed in 2020 after the country called for an independent investigation into the source of COVID-19.

Don't think this can happen only in smaller countries. A Tibetan from a prominent family, whom I will call Dorje, was living and studying in New York a few years ago. This young student was not especially political, but he had met with the Dalai Lama and those around him and had been involved in a project that likely caused the Chinese to regard him as a political figure. One day, while he was waiting for a bus in Queens, he was approached by a fellow Tibetan. After confirming Dorje's identity, the Tibetan asked him to come around the corner to talk further. There, a Han Chinese threatened him verbally not to talk in public and destroyed his phone. The incident emotionally scarred Dorje. He did not report it to police. The threats had the result the Chinese wanted: Dorje has gone quiet.

I was intrigued to note the indictment and arrest in 2020 of Baimadajie Angwang, an ethnically Tibetan New York City policeman on charges that he worked with mainland officials in New York to provide intel and assist them in recruiting agents. One of the mainland officials Angwang acted for was employed by the China Association for Preservation and Development of Tibetan Culture, part of the mainland's United Front Work Department. "The Department was responsible for neutralizing potential opponents of the PRC and co-opting ethnic Chinese individuals living outside the PRC," according to the indictment charging Angwang with acting as an illegal agent.

Lam Wing-kee, the arrested bookseller whose description of his own arrest exposed the mainland involvement in the abduction, moved to Taiwan in April 2019, after the controversial extradition bill that would spark the 2019 demonstrations was proposed. Even in Taiwan, Lam was harassed by pro-mainlanders. When he tried to open a Taiwan version of Causeway Bay Books, he was sued, unsuccessfully, for copyright infringement. Then, shortly before the store opened, Lam was splashed with red paint. The attention he received from pro-mainland thugs has seemingly only strengthened his resolve and raised the new bookstore's profile. After the opening of Causeway Bay Books's Taiwan branch, President Tsai Ing-wen paid a visit to the store and wrote a message of support: "Taiwan stands for Hong Kong's freedom."

So far, we've looked at the increasingly assertive attempts of Hong Kongers to protect the city's free way of life in the years after 1997, as China proved unwilling to allow convincing moves toward genuine universal suffrage. But any account of this struggle also needs to look at the role of the territory's government and business elite in frustrating the ambitions of the enclave's people and in ultimately opening the way for unchecked Communist rule. Most of the princes, and princesses, of government and business not only failed to stand up for the former colony's freedoms but acquiesced in, and often profited from, policies that cemented the power of entrenched interests, especially by allowing super-profits to be skimmed from the real estate sector. This fueled the popular, democratic protests.

FOUR

PROPERTY AND POVERTY

Hong Kong is a city that once made real things, from toys and tofu to sweaters and shirts. But as manufacturing moved to Southern China in the 1980s and '90s, Hong Kong started making something else: property millionaires and property billionaires. With steep hills rising from a deep natural harbor, Hong Kong has a shortage of flat land that can easily be built upon; this posed a challenge from the colony's earliest days. Building sites were mostly on slopes or land that had been clawed back from the sea in expensive and environmentally damaging reclamation projects.

Hong Kong's land problem was exacerbated by the handover negotiations in the early 1980s. As with so much in Hong Kong, Chinese suspicion of Britain led to problems. The Chinese worried that the British were going to try to siphon off Hong Kong's wealth for themselves before 1997. There were rumors that secret tunnels had been dug from the Hongkong and Shanghai Banking Corporation headquarters in Central District to the harbor, allegedly so that gold and cash could be spirited out of the colony. Selling land cheaply to British buyers in the run-up to the handover would be an obvious strategy to enrich the outgoing colonists and their friends. The Chinese were haunted by the idea that Britain would wreck Hong Kong before leaving and wanted to ensure that property wasn't handed out in sweetheart deals.

Chinese concerns resulted in an agreement under the 1984 Sino-British Joint Declaration to limit land leases to 50 hectares (123 acres) a year until the 1997 handover. (Land is leased, usually for fifty years, rather than sold outright in Hong Kong.) That is a little more than twice the size of the 55-acre Great Lawn in New York City's Central Park. The limit was imposed at a time when property prices had slumped following the spectacular 1983 collapse of the Carrian Group, whose debt-fueled acquisition binge had produced a property bubble in the colony. Deep uncertainty about what would happen after 1997 kept demand for new property subdued. Even so, 50 hectares of land wasn't much in a city of 5.4 million people. Over time, the constraint proved to be about as sensible as telling a five-year-old boy that he needed to wear the same size shoes for the next fifteen years. Problems appeared even before the end of the 1980s. China Light and Power's Lawrence Kadoorie went straight to Beijing to get an exemption so that he could build a new multi-hectare electricity plant at Black Point (much to the unhappiness of British authorities, remembers his son, Michael).[1]

When the Chinese economy boomed after Deng Xiaoping's reforms took root, the fifty-hectare limit proved to be a straitjacket. Land prices rose sharply. Land-lease revenues in turn swelled government coffers, so the government had an incentive to ensure that prices stayed high. The high prices also enriched the small group of property developers able to pay hundreds of millions of dollars up front for projects that would not start generating a return for years. Although it cost money to hold on to the land, the deep-pocketed developers got a double benefit: they profited from rising real estate values as well as from the apartments they developed on a site. This sort of land hoarding was especially true of agricultural land that was bought cheaply and converted to more profitable residential property.

The tight supply of land persisted even after the 1997 handover, as the government and property developers benefited too much to allow prices to fall. Despite Hong Kong's small size, large developers Sun Hung Kai Properties and Henderson Land Development are among the world's most profitable and highly valued real estate companies.[2] The high land-price policy also helped prepare the ground for the political upheavals of 2014 and 2019 by making it impossible for half the population to buy a home.

In conversations after the handover, Chinese officials invoked Marxist doctrine to assert that Hong Kong was a business city. According to their distorted version of Marxism, which says history progresses in stages, Hong Kong was in a period of capitalist revolution. On this simplistic analysis, keeping business happy became a reflex. Hence, the close ties between Hong Kong's government and the city's business tycoons can be understood in light of this perversion of traditional Marxist doctrine, a sinister twist on what the Chinese call their economy—"socialism with Chinese characteristics." This was particularly evident with regard to property, where the government and a handful of large family-controlled developers worked to keep supply restricted and ensure that prices rebounded to a high level after the 1997–98 Asian financial crisis. It is ironic that a Communist country has grafted a conservative nineteenth-century laissez-faire attitude onto its rule, enabling billionaires to be minted on a world-class scale. The links between government and business, and the distortions introduced into Hong Kong's traditionally laissez-faire economy, largely stem from this reliance on up-front land-lease payments and a policy of restricting supply.

Just how expensive is Hong Kong property? One yardstick compares how long an average income earner needs to work to buy a typical property. In Hong Kong, it takes more than twenty years of earnings for the average person to buy an apartment, about four times the ratio in New York or London, places that are hardly known for their easily affordable property. (This was before the pandemic—Hong Kong's property prices fell less in 2020 than New York's and London's.) My former *BusinessWeek* colleague Frederik Balfour wrote an article comparing the interior space for a typical Hong Kong apartment with a Tesla Model X. "You Could Barely Squeeze a Tesla into This $500K Apartment," read the headline on Balfour's story about a

161-square-foot apartment sold by Henderson Land. Try measuring your bathroom to get a sense of the size; if it's a master bathroom in a typical new American home, it's larger than this $500,000 apartment.[3] In Hong Kong, a parking space can cost even more. In 2017, one sold for a record $664,300. That record doubled to $1.3 million in 2021.[4] Parking spaces are now just another target for Hong Kong investors. Leased out for a few hundred dollars a month, they generate regular income, have virtually no maintenance costs, and tend to appreciate over time.

Parking lot speculators represent one stereotype of Hong Kongers as money-obsessed. As a colony that was perched precariously on the edge of China (summed up in the title of Richard Hughes's book *Borrowed Place, Borrowed Time*), Hong Kong has always been about making money. From the high finance of Central, home to Asia's international financial hub, to closet-size computer components shops in Sham Shui Po's Golden Arcade shopping center, the city hums with entrepreneurial verve. The stereotype has more than a kernel of truth in what was long a refugee city. People work hard, and there is a hustling energy in the air.

A new, less money-oriented aspect of Hong Kong has developed in the past decade, a change that the city's elite hasn't understood, let alone accepted. During the 2014 Umbrella Movement, it became apparent that many Hong Kong millennials, born in the years just before the handover, rejected this money-first ethos. "It is just weird to want to spend your whole life to earn for a small apartment when for the same money you could get a nice place with a huge garden somewhere else," Chan, one of my Cantonese teachers, told me. (He was born in 1991.) "People in Hong Kong and China value real estate. They say if you want to get a girlfriend, get a house first. Real estate is a life goal." Like many of his peers, Chan plans to leave Hong Kong when pandemic restrictions ease.

Hong Kong is often ranked as the world's freest economy, as it was for nearly three decades beginning in the 1990s, by the conservative U.S. think tank the Heritage Foundation, before being dropped from the list in 2021 because it was no longer seen as autonomous. The ranking reflects, above all, low tax rates and a simple tax system.

It is ironic that a free-market American organization would celebrate an economy that has strong socialist elements. A city where half the population lives in public housing and where residents enjoy low-cost universal medical care does not exemplify laissez-faire capitalism.

Land sales fund a low-tax paradise. Besides the 15 percent salary tax and 16.5 percent corporate profits tax, there are few other levies—no social security taxes, no Medicare or unemployment levies. There is no sales tax. Estate taxes were eliminated in 2005, and Hong Kong became an increasingly important private banking center as wealthy Asians moved their assets into the territory. Even the tax on wine was eliminated in 2008, making Hong Kong one of the only major economies in the world with a zero-tax wine policy. This change quickly led to its also becoming one of the world's largest wine markets. Its land revenues are so large that Hong Kong has, until the 2020 pandemic, run budget surpluses for most of the previous half century. These surpluses are so large that the government is embarrassed into giving money back to Hong Kongers. Tax rebates are common. Some years, it just gives cash—HK$6,000 ($769) in 2012 and HK$10,000 ($1,282) in 2020—to all permanent residents.

Its treatment of property makes Hong Kong's economic system unique. The government gets almost half its revenues from its upfront land premiums.[5] (Property taxes, a common source of recurring tax revenue in many countries, are tiny in Hong Kong.) The proceeds from land sales go into the Capital Works Reserve Fund, which is used to build more infrastructure that, in turn, makes property more valuable and further enriches developers. Besides the coterie of developers, a pair of government-controlled companies play important roles. The MTR, which operates the city's excellent mass transit rail system, is publicly traded on the Stock Exchange of Hong Kong but is controlled by the government (as is the Exchange), which owns 75 percent of the company. The MTR is profitable, but not because of its subway system. The government grants the rail operator the development rights to the area around its stations, allowing the MTR to build apartment blocks and shopping centers, which it then profitably rents out or sells. Think of the MTR as a property developer masquerading as a public transit company, one with preferential access to new development sites that are guaranteed to succeed by virtue of the rail and subway lines the company itself is building.

Hong Kong's property policy has produced exceptional income inequality. Hong Kong has more billionaires per capita than almost anyplace on earth. Research firm Wealth-X's 2019 Billionaire Census report counted eighty-seven billionaires in Hong Kong (collectively worth $259 billion), ranking the city of 7.5 million people seventh in the world in number of billionaires, just behind Switzerland and ahead of India.

Billionaires aside, about 1.3 million people, one sixth of the population, live below the poverty line. With a minimum wage of less than $5 an hour, the median monthly salary is less than $2,000, which means that half the working population makes less than $24,000 a year. Hong Kong's income inequality is the most pronounced among all prosperous societies, far worse than that of the United States, worse even than that of Zimbabwe and many poor countries. Damning though these statistics are, they would be far worse if wealth (the value of property, stocks, bonds, savings, and other assets) were included in these calculations.

Even the working poor cannot afford to rent a decent place on the open market. Only a large-scale public housing program makes this policy of deliberately high property prices and low wages possible. Almost half the population lives in public housing. Tens of thousands more live in caged homes (where each person's space in a large dormitory room is enclosed in a cage, to guard against theft) or apartments that are subdivided to squeeze families of four or five people into less than one hundred square feet.

I visited one of these subdivided flats in Sham Shui Po, a crowded working-class district, on a sweltering August day. I was joined by a colleague and an interpreter—there simply wasn't room for anyone else in our group in the one-hundred-square-foot apartment, which, though smaller than an average American bathroom, was home to a couple, their elementary school–age children, and an aging parent. The mother and father clearly wanted and hoped for their children to have good schooling opportunities. The engaged and alert boy and girl appeared grateful for our visit, for we represented a sign that someone cared. But the odds were that the children would not rise to the top of Hong Kong's hypercompetitive, exam-based educational system and would therefore not go to university. Instead, they were likely to languish in menial, low-paying, unskilled jobs. Per square foot, the family paid the same rent as one would for a luxury apartment (about $77 per square foot per year); monthly rent was $641, about 40 percent of their $1,500 monthly income. The family still needed to pay for food, bus and subway fares, and their children's educational expenses.

They were by no means the worst off. One woman I met, living in an apartment provided by a Christian charity, had for a time been living with her husband in a tent on Butterfly Beach. The beach on the city's northwestern coast is home to several dozen of the city's working poor, who cluster in a makeshift encampment. After her husband lost his job because of an illness, they had been forced to move out of their apartment; although she had part-time housework, it didn't pay enough to cover rent. With no effective welfare system to provide a safety net, and a long wait for public housing, they were reduced to living on the beach.

The situation gets more difficult and degrading for those who don't work. Rendered homeless, whether from illness (often mental illness) or drug addiction, clusters of indigent people gather in parks in Sham Shui Po and other areas. I visited one of these with Jeff Rotmeyer, a Canadian who in 2013 founded the NGO ImpactHK, to help street sleepers. We met at the ImpactHK sports center on Bedford Street—nearby streets were Larch, Lime, Willow, Walnut, Maple, Cedar, and Sycamore, the names a reminder of the British colonial past in an area of Hong Kong just south of Boundary Street (the colony's northernmost border until the New Territories were taken by the United Kingdom in 1898, in the wake of the Second Convention of Peking).

Hundreds of people live outside in the 5.5-hectare Tung Chau Street Park, some too sick even to acknowledge us as we distributed bananas, eggs, and water. I handed out bananas and then poured water for people, who often just grabbed the food. One pair of men readied a shared syringe before first one and then the other injected (heroin, most likely, though methamphetamine, or "ice," is also common). Rotmeyer told me that most people who are on the street have no family. Hong Kong has one of the world's lowest fertility rates; on average, each woman has only one child. As the city ages further, and family size continues to shrink, this problem will only increase.

The park is next to a raised highway that leads to the airport, with its connections to the rest of the world, but these people aren't going anywhere. Towering new apartment blocks—easily more than $1 billion in real estate—overlook the attractive park, with its lush trees and an octagonal pavilion set in the center of an artificial pond. This is one of a handful of parks in Hong Kong that stay open all night so that people can freely sleep there. There are some government shelters—in fact, there is one about 150 yards from the park, but it is open only when there are warnings for very hot or very cold weather or a typhoon. Rotmeyer, a curly-haired man in his mid-thirties, aims to give street sleepers the self-confidence and organizational skills to be able to live in the apartments ImpactHK finds for them.

Hundreds of people who would rather not sleep outside pass the nights in McDonald's restaurant outlets, a phenomenon that spawned the term "McRefugee," as well as a 2018 movie *I'm Livin' It*, the title a riff on the McDonald's slogan "I'm Lovin' It." After restaurants had to close at 6 p.m. because of COVID-19 restrictions in 2020, as many as 500 McRefugees were thrown onto the streets. In response, ImpactHK accelerated the housing hunt and, by late 2020, was housing more than 150 people a night, mostly at guesthouses.

❧

Two stories about Hong Kong buildings illustrate the lust for extra profit and the pervasive craziness of the Hong Kong property market. Looming over the surrounding cityscape near the eastern end of Hong Kong Island stands the Grand Promenade housing complex, five towers ranging in height from sixty-one to sixty-four stories. With 2,020 apartments in the complex, this is one of the mega-projects of the sort that Hong Kong's property developers have come to favor since the 1997 handover. The upmarket complex—a 1,500-square-foot apartment was listed in late 2020 for nearly

$7.2 million—stands out from the scruffy working-class neighborhood that surrounds it. The Grand Promenade became notorious by benefiting from the sort of bureaucratic discretion that is not supposed to exist in law-abiding, corruption-free Hong Kong.

During the go-go days in the 1950s and '60s, the colony had been notoriously corrupt, a condition that provided fuel for riots in 1966. The rot reached into senior ranks of the police force. Only a determined campaign by 1970s governor Murray MacLehose saw the government clean house. The cleanup went ahead despite an uprising during which protesting policemen surrounded the headquarters of the newly created Independent Commission Against Corruption. The ICAC, a super-body that reported to the governor, was a source of pride for many in the city, though its effectiveness—at least as measured by high-profile cases—has faded since the handover. Ties between the government and developers are one area where Hong Kong's clean image has been called into question.

The Grand Promenade project was one that raised such questions. Henderson Land won the tender for the site with a land premium of $311 million in January 2001. Then it engaged in a technical maneuver that allowed it to build more apartments by getting the government to exclude a public bus terminus that it was required to build from the overall calculation of the project's square footage. In the end, Henderson boosted the gross floor area of the Grand Promenade project to 135,451 square meters (up from the original plan of 85,720 square meters) and doubled the number of apartments in the five residential blocks from 1,008 to 2,020. The additional 50,000 square meters increased Henderson's revenue by roughly $64 million. (The change in status for the bus terminus alone resulted in an additional 20,000 square meters; other changes allowed it to reach the additional 50,000 square meters.) By the government's own calculation, the change allowed Henderson to save $16 million in land premiums. The key official in the decision soon retired; he then went to work for a number of real estate companies, though none were Henderson-linked.

Another project, also developed by Henderson, was built a few years later, on Conduit Road, in Hong Kong's expensive Mid-Levels district. Construction continued during the 2008–9 financial crisis, and I wondered if pricing would remain high.

The first hint that something might be amiss with 39 Conduit Road came with the news that a penthouse on the building's sixty-eighth floor had sold for almost $57 million. The price worked out to $11,350 a square foot, well above the average for the neighborhood.[6] It wasn't just that this was expensive; it was that Henderson was selling a sixty-eighth-story penthouse in a forty-story building! Next came the news that the eighty-eighth-floor penthouse was up for sale. It was, in fact, one floor above the so-called sixty-eighth-floor penthouse. It's common to omit the fourth and the thirteenth floors, four being an unlucky number in Chinese and thirteen unlucky in English. But to leave out more than forty floors? This took development shenanigans to new heights.[7]

Henderson was headed by a billionaire named Lee Shau-kee, who had grown rich through his control of the colony's gas company, Hong Kong and China Gas, known simply as Towngas. Chinese generally don't like to cook on electric stoves—it is hard to get the needed heat for wok-fired foods—and virtually every family sent Towngas a monthly payment. The utility was a monopoly provider, and it was unregulated, so it had the freedom to charge whatever customers would pay. Lee took his earnings from the stable, recession-proof gas business and put much of it into property. In deference to his use of a stable business that reliably threw off large amounts of cash that could be used in more speculative investments, the Hong Kong press called him the Warren Buffett of Asia. Commenting on the misnumbered floors, he said, "Buyers like those numbers, and we aren't cheating them."[8]

Given that the price was about 50 percent higher than comparable properties in the area, it appeared that the company might be trying to secretly push up the market. Following a public outcry, Hong Kong authorities quizzed the buyers. Mainland media reported that one of them was a Shanxi businesswoman named Ding Yuxin, who bought three of the units for $45 million. Ding, originally known as Ding Shumiao, was notorious for her relationship with one of China's most corrupt officials, railways minister Liu Zhijun. Both Ding and Liu were arrested in 2011. Ding was said to have taken kickbacks of $67 million; Liu was plotting to buy his way on to the Chinese Communist Party's Central Committee and eventually the Politburo, bodies that are at the core of Chinese power.[9] Liu was sentenced to prison for stealing tens of millions of dollars; Hong Kong's *Ming Pao* newspaper reported that he had eighteen mistresses. Ding, who began her business career as an illiterate egg seller, was imprisoned as his accomplice.

The Conduit Road apartment story now appeared more complicated than it looked at first glance. Rather than price manipulation, the speculation became that the prices were driven by mainland money launderers. One could imagine that players like Ding wanted to get money out of the mainland. Hong Kong has long been a preferred place for mainland Chinese to stash assets, ill-gotten or otherwise, which are often routed through difficult-to-trace shell companies in the British Virgin Islands. Hong Kong is close enough to China, but its independent and autonomous legal system shielded those assets from mainland authorities—or at least they did until recently. People who want to hide assets are often willing to pay a premium; put another way, they aren't in a strong position to bargain. Getting the money to a safe haven is often more important than haggling over the last dollar.

Even Hong Kong's prized reputation for clean government could not withstand the temptations that the property market presented. Rafael Hui was the number two official under Chief Executive Donald Tsang from 2005 to 2007. He received Hong Kong's highest awards, the Grand Bauhinia Medal and the Gold Bauhinia Star (part of a wide-ranging system that unironically mimicked the British queen's Birthday Honours list, even down to the last detail of its being announced on the anniversary of the establishment of the Hong Kong Special Administrative Region). Hui was convicted of taking more than $1 million in bribes from the controlling family and senior executives of the Sun Hung Kai property company, one of the big property developers. He had been the financial services secretary under Chris Patten and was widely regarded as one of the smartest and most capable officials of his generation.

Nicknamed "Fat Dragon," Hui had an increasingly ample girth, a testament to the vitello tonnato and other rich foods I knew he favored from the time I'd hosted him for lunches at the Grand Hyatt Hotel's Grissini restaurant and at Da Domenico, a modest-looking but expensive Italian restaurant favored by Hong Kong's elite. (We'd been introduced when I was the publisher and editor in chief of *The Standard* by the newspaper's owner, Charles Ho.) Besides good food, Hui loved opera and boasted of his trips to Europe to enjoy both. He was smart, and he was cynical—at our first lunch, he told me he would take a lump-sum payout of his pension, rather than recurring payouts, because he thought that the Hong Kong government was entering a period of deficits that would put pensions at jeopardy. (In fact, *surpluses* over the next fifteen years soared to embarrassingly high levels.)

Hui prided himself on hinting at his ties to leaders in Beijing, and he was fond of resorting to vague threats by alluding to the "sovereign power." Once, he issued a warning to me that the United States was pushing so hard on a Taiwan issue that it could mean crossing a red line and raising the possibility of conflict. It seemed he thought I would pass this warning on to contacts he imagined I had in the U.S. or British governments. The most ludicrous invocation of Beijing's influence came when Hui warned me while I was editor in chief at the *South China Morning Post* that if the newspaper supported Earth Day, with its symbolic and largely meaningless gesture of switching lights off for an hour, this would be seen as a challenge to the "sovereign power," the Chinese government.

I had wondered at Hui's decision to stay in his existing apartment when he was appointed as chief secretary. The chief secretary's official house, perched high on the Peak, boasted its own tennis court, spectacular gardens, and stunning views of the harbor. In a city with many beautiful views of the harbor, the house had among the best. Meanwhile, Hui's apartment was in the Leighton Hill complex, on the edge of Happy Valley, a former swamp that had been turned into a racecourse. Without thinking about it too much, I figured that Hui was more comfortable in his own apartment. Later, it was revealed that the apartment wasn't his, but had been provided to him by Sun Hung Kai executives, along with cash, in return for his agreeing to be their eyes and ears in government while he headed the Mandatory Provident Fund (the government pension scheme), as chief secretary, and finally when serving in the chief executive's cabinet, the Executive Council.

Hui's ill-gotten remuneration financed his sybaritic lifestyle, which included not only vitello tonnato and opera but also a mistress. He was sentenced to seven and a half years in prison—he served five—and ordered to return $1.4 million in bribes received while he was on the Executive Council. A jury found him not guilty of accepting other bribes totaling more than $2 million during the time he headed the Mandatory Provident Fund and was chief secretary. This man was among the best and brightest in Hong Kong, one who had reached the pinnacle of Hong Kong's civil service, had occupied key financial and political positions, and received the territory's highest awards. Disgraced, he became a symbol of a corrupt, cynical elite intent on pleasing Beijing and grabbing what it could for itself.

Hui was exceptional in his greed and in his half-hearted attempts to cover up his crimes. But the contempt and the cynicism he displayed toward the territory's people and the cravenness he displayed toward Beijing were reflected throughout much of the elite. The upper crust's contempt for working-class Hong Kongers coupled with deference to a distant power (whether in London or Beijing) represented a long-standing failure to understand that ordinary Hong Kongers' respect for hard work, a sense of fair play, and a belief in competent administration set the city apart. Yet, to fully understand just why, and by how much, the former colony has deteriorated, we must look deeper into its past.

PART II

"BORROWED PLACE, BORROWED TIME"

FIVE

OPIUM, FREE TRADE, AND A "BARREN ROCK"

Colonial Hong Kong was a city of freedom founded on a crime. It was a place of refuge that suffered from its colonial taint. It was a safe lockbox for profits made in the China trade that benefited from China's weakness. Hong Kong was a British Crown colony, ruled by a monarch half a world away whose troops had seized it in a war. The roots of this conquest are important, for they underpin the Chinese Communist Party's narrative today.

What became known as the First Opium War was launched in 1839, after a group of British merchants complained that their opium—which was illegal in China—had been confiscated by Chinese authorities without compensation. The British launched the war to retaliate but justified it on the broader grounds that China should open up to trade with the outside world, despite the opposition of the Chinese government. Britain demanded free trade at the barrel of a gun, engaging, literally, in gunboat diplomacy for the sake of drug trafficking.

For China in the second half of the nineteenth century, British possession of Hong Kong was an irritant rather than a serious problem, as the Qing dynasty struggled to survive before finally collapsing in 1911. China's powerlessness led to a hands-off attitude toward Hong Kong that continued for the first half of the twentieth century, a period in which Communists and Nationalists fought a civil war for control of the world's most populous country.

The First Opium War initiated a series of conflicts that saw scores of colonies, treaty ports, and extraterritorial zones—where Chinese law did not apply—set up in China by Britain, France, Germany, Russia, and Japan. China, complained nineteenth-century nationalists, was "carved up like a melon." Hong Kong Island was occupied in 1841, although negotiations to end the First Opium War concluded only in August 1842. The settlement of the Second Opium War, fought in the late 1850s, allowed Britain to increase the size of the colony to include parts of mainland Kowloon. The Second Opium War was largely fought in Northern China and culminated in British and French troops pillaging the imperial Summer Palace in Beijing.

Then, in 1898, Britain forced China to accept a ninety-nine-year lease of Hong Kong's so-called New Territories, which increased the colony's size twelvefold, making it a bit larger than today's New York City. With the acquisition of the New Territories, the British Crown colony pushed deeper into the Chinese mainland. The New Territories lease would expire on June 30, 1997. It was this "fateful" date, as 1950s governor Alexander Grantham called it, that prompted Margaret Thatcher's agreement to hand the territory back to China. Although Hong Kong Island and the southern tip of Kowloon had been ceded in perpetuity, it would be almost impossible to defend Hong Kong militarily. The dividing line between the New Territories and the rest of Hong Kong ran through Kai Tak Airport. Hong Kong depended on China for most of its food and much of its water. Halfway around the world from Britain, if faced with a hostile China, Hong Kong could not be supplied like West Berlin during the Cold War, when an airlift kept the city free.

Hong Kong was a place that harbored and helped save the lives of revolutionaries who would go on to play pivotal roles in the founding of modern China, Vietnam, and the Philippines. Sun Yat-sen, the father of modern China, studied medicine at what later became the University of Hong Kong—the city's first university, designed to support reform in China. In 1923, Sun told students at the university that it was corruption in China and the peace, order, and good government of Hong Kong that had turned him into a revolutionary.

> More than thirty years ago I was studying in Hong Kong and spent a great deal of spare time in walking the streets of the Colony. Hong Kong impressed me a great deal, because there was orderly calm and because there was artistic work being done without interruption. I went to my home in Heungshan twice a year and immediately noticed the great difference. There was disorder instead of order, insecurity instead of security. . . .

❀

> I compared [my hometown of] Heungshan with Hong Kong and, although they are only 50 miles apart, the difference of the Governments impressed me very much. Afterwards, I saw the outside world and I began to wonder how it was that foreigners, that Englishmen[,] could do such things as they had done, for example, with the barren rock of Hong Kong, within 70 or 80 years, while China, in 4,000 years, had no places like Hong Kong.[1]

The notion of Hong Kong as a place of safety and refuge, one where new political and social ideas could be promoted in a Chinese society, is one that continues to resonate. For a century and a half of British rule, Hong Kong was a Chinese place but one that was free of the Chinese government.

After José Rizal, the Philippines' founding father, angered the country's Spanish colonial rulers, he took refuge in Hong Kong. The city became home in the following years to a number of Filipino revolutionaries. Ho Chi Minh, the father of modern Vietnam, arrived under a pseudonym in 1930 and worked as an underground organizer for the Vietnamese Communist Party. He was arrested by Hong Kong colonial authorities and held for extradition to Vietnam. His lawyer argued that police had arrested Ho without a warrant. In a case that went to London's Privy Council, Ho won release.[2] His experience shows the importance of the rule of law in Hong Kong. The 2019 demonstrations began as a protest against a law that would have, for the first time, stripped away Hong Kong's status as an enclave protected from the arbitrary Chinese legal system.

The colony was also plagued by racism, social snobbery, and anti-Semitism; self-satisfied and parochial, Hong Kong before 1945 would barely have ranked as a second-rate British coastal town. Prominent businessman Lawrence Kadoorie, born in 1899 to an Iraqi-Jewish family active in both Hong Kong and Shanghai, was dismissive of early twentieth-century Hong Kong. In reflecting on the prewar period, Kadoorie scoffed that the colony "was very insular" in the 1920s, "not international like Shanghai." It was "very much a small provincial town. I have often compared the two to Shanghai being London and Hong Kong being more like Hastings or Eastbourne at most," he said, referring to two southeastern English seaside towns in the area where he attended high school.[3]

Hong Kong was an overwhelmingly Chinese city, but in the nineteenth century, Chinese needed passes if they ventured outdoors at night. They were subjected to a variety of other racial humiliations. They could not live in the exclusive Peak district or even in the less exclusive Mid-Levels area. Social life in Hong Kong, as in other British colonies, revolved around private clubs; yet Chinese could not join any of the city's most exclusive recreational or social clubs—the Jockey Club, the Hong Kong Club, the Ladies Recreation Club, or the Royal Hong Kong Yacht Club—until well after the end of World War II. The prewar era was an age of pompous "blimps" (a Briticism for pompous, reactionary persons), wrote Governor Alexander Grantham, who had served as a young cadet in the colony. When the Japanese invaded Hong Kong in December 1941, a few hours after their attack on Pearl Harbor, the British agonized over whether they could trust any local Chinese with weapons.[4] The age of the "blimps" may have passed, but much of the small-mindedness remained in the first decades after World War II. When Grantham hosted a dinner for the visiting actress Elizabeth Taylor and her husband Michael Todd at his Government House residence, he felt compelled to conceal from his Hong Kong guests the fact that Todd was Jewish.

Hong Kong's establishment as a British Crown colony broke the stranglehold on trade with China imposed by the Qing dynasty. No longer would traders be restricted to a six-month presence in Canton (today's Guangzhou), during which they were confined to their quarters and had to employ Chinese go-betweens to do business. Hong Kong took over much of the role that Canton had enjoyed. This was entrepôt capitalism; opium was shipped to Hong Kong before being smuggled into China, while tea, silks, and porcelain came from China to Hong Kong en route to the rest of the world. Opium sales were justified by the British partly as a way of evening out the unfavorable balance of trade. The start of large-scale opium trade in the 1820s and '30s helped reverse what had been a serious drain on Britain's silver reserves stemming from the fact that Britain bought tea, silk, porcelain, and other Chinese products but sold little in return. China did not want much from the world—or, so said the government. The British thought the imbalance was due to restrictions on trade, and they were determined to pry open the market, even if it meant war.

Hong Kong would develop into a little patch of Britain, its security and civil liberties unknown in the rest of China, reassuring to both businessmen—Chinese, British, Americans, and others—and ordinary Chinese. Yet the territory was derided as a "barren rock with nary a house upon it" by British foreign secretary Lord Palmerston upon his hearing of its acquisition. Palmerston had hoped to acquire more promising territory as a result of winning the Opium War. Promptly dismissing Capt. Charles Elliot, who had taken possession of the island in January 1841 and had agreed in subsequent negotiations to end the war, Palmerston intoned that Hong Kong "will never be a mart for trade." So much for predictions.[5]

An aggressive opium trader named William Jardine played a leading role in initiating the Opium War. Called the Iron-Headed Old Rat by one of his Chinese interlocutors, Jardine successfully lobbied for war—even supplying detailed plans for the military campaign. He and his firm, Jardine Matheson, exploited the ugly side of colonialism, enlisting the power of the British military to facilitate their drug trafficking.

It was as if drug lord Pablo Escobar's Medellín cartel, angered by the seizure of its cocaine in Southern California, persuaded Colombia to invade the United States, seize San Diego County in perpetuity, and use it as a protected base for its drug-smuggling operations. Or as if China seized the San Francisco Bay Area and set up a thriving trading and smuggling hub with operations throughout the United States, but beyond the reach of U.S. authorities.

Opium was illegal in China but a staple of Hong Kong's economy. Inside the colony, the government derived substantial revenues well into the twentieth century by auctioning off the monopoly right to sell opium locally in Hong Kong. Opium smoking in Hong Kong was outlawed only in the 1940s; the government ended its monopoly on sales of the drug in 1945. The drug was central to Hong Kong as a British colony. Many Hong Kong fortunes were made thanks to opium, by British, Parsees (from Bombay), and Americans. Revenues from opium sales tilted the balance of trade with China in Britain's favor.[6]

For China, the seizure of Hong Kong represents the beginning of a century of humiliation, during which a proud civilization was subjected to degrading treatment by Europeans, Americans, and Japanese. China's current government has nurtured this sense of national grievance for its own purposes, but it is nonetheless real. Westerners too often ignore the way in which the memory of colonial Hong Kong symbolizes China's sense of wounded pride and injured dignity. Deng Xiaoping's statement to Margaret Thatcher that the Chinese could run Hong Kong just fine but, if they didn't, so be it, comes from the sense of national pride at recovering stolen territory.

The attitude of British and other Westerners to Hong Kong and its people was tinged with racism and condescension, an affliction few colonies escape—its effects can still be felt to this day. I have heard countless casually racist remarks, but it is small incidents relating to the language, and to the distance that expatriates kept from Hong Kong by refusing even to try learning Cantonese, that stick out in my mind. My daughter's British-based elementary school switched its second language from French to Mandarin (forget about Cantonese) only immediately before the 1997 handover. A few years later,

I asked a friend whose husband was one of the most powerful expatriates in Hong Kong and who had lived there for the better part of twenty years if she spoke Cantonese: "Oh, heavens, no!" came the answer, as if a white woman speaking the language would be unpardonable in polite company.

China has tapped into deep and understandable resentment at a century and a half of colonial domination during which the people of Hong Kong were not in control. "Hong Kong was built and made prosperous on the blood, sweat, and corpses of Chinese coolies," intoned a 1958 book published in Beijing. This narrative, notes journalist and historian Vaudine England, "is all about British aggression, discrimination, exploitation."[7]

The Chinese Communist Party uses this sense of wounded national pride to strengthen its legitimacy. Weeks before Hong Kong's 1997 handover to China, incoming chief executive Tung Chee-hwa and other pro-Beijing dignitaries watched *The Opium War*, a Chinese movie whose director likened Queen Victoria's Britain to Hitler's Third Reich. Outgoing governor Chris Patten was not invited. His press secretary said that he was more interested in objective history than propaganda and had recently watched *The Gate of Heavenly Peace*, a documentary about the 1989 Tiananmen killings.[8]

The British long downplayed the imperial violence that had given birth to Hong Kong and emphasized softer, more positive aspects of colonial rule, such as economic prosperity, the rule of law, good governance, and a strong economy. Generations of Hong Kong schoolchildren learned that the First Anglo-Chinese War, as the Opium War was officially called, was about free trade.[9]

In different circumstances, the British Crown colony of Hong Kong might have been an independent city-state, similar to Singapore. Given that it is geographically part of China, the odds were always against this. From the Chinese perspective—and this was one point on which the Nationalists and the Communist Chinese agreed—the fact that Hong Kong had become a British colony was a historical wrong that would someday be righted by its restoration to China.

From the colony's earliest days, local Chinese business leaders also flourished, despite racial barriers. A group of Chinese and Eurasian go-betweens, known as compradors, navigated between Western and Chinese worlds and acted as guarantors for the two sides of a transaction. Robert Hotung, the comprador for Jardine Matheson, spoke English and Chinese. Hotung became the first of the truly wealthy Chinese, but there were many others, both compradors and merchants. The British allowed room for a local commercial elite to flourish, to grow wealthy, and to enjoy more personal freedom and protection of property rights than they would have been granted in China. In China, merchants were seen as second-class citizens, subject to the whims of the local magistrate, if not the emperor himself.[10]

Chinese business leaders were the main conduit for relaying the sentiments of an overwhelmingly Cantonese city to British colonial authorities. The business elite unsurprisingly held a conservative attitude, one that favored stability, property rights, and commercial success over notions of social welfare, workers' rights, or civil liberties. The merchant elite occupied a tenuous position, straddling as they did the world of international commerce and the Chinese community they were supposed to represent. Colonial authorities relied on Chinese merchants both for their knowledge of the Chinese populace and to enforce British colonial policies in that world. This system was flawed, for the interests of the elite were quite different from those of workers. Merchants were apt to disparage concerns of the mass of workers—the "ignorant people," as one Chinese newspaper called them—the coolies, rickshaw pullers, dockworkers, and the like who made up most of the city's population.[11]

The colonial authorities' dependence on Chinese businessmen set a pattern that has persisted to this day; a Chinese elite, out of touch with grassroots opinion, serves as a primary source of information, much of it flawed, about the Chinese world. It would be wrong to say that these merchants had no more interest in the welfare of their fellow Chinese than the British did. They founded charitable institutions, notably the Tung Wah group of hospitals.[12] But it is true that Hong Kong was a colonial business city, one where the business elite—be it British, Chinese, Indian, Jewish, or Armenian—had an extraordinary degree of political power. This power was directed toward making as much money as quickly as possible; relatively little energy was devoted to dealing with social issues, especially given Hong Kong's floating population. It was a colony where people moved across the border with Guangdong in search of work, leaving when times were tough in Hong Kong, a place where, every year, tens of thousands arrived before shipping out to California or the tin mines of Malaysia or other places in search of their fortune. Europe and America had progressive social movements in the late nineteenth and early twentieth centuries that fought for better working conditions; such movements were squelched in Hong Kong, as in most colonies. After 1945, most colonies enjoyed liberation and independence. Hong Kong would not.

Chinese working-class districts in the nineteenth century were characterized by dark, airless dwellings and narrow, excrement-filled lanes. Night soil was removed by hand, in buckets, a practice that lasted in some neighborhoods until the late twentieth century. In a scathing 1882 report, Victorian-era health expert Osbert Chadwick recommended sweeping reforms: the construction of water mains and sewers and the enactment of better building codes. The report accomplished very little. Chinese and British merchants alike fought the introduction of mandatory building and sanitation codes. It was only after bubonic plague came to Hong Kong in 1895, prompting many workers to flee across the border, that sanitation reforms were grudgingly instituted. Even then, the business community fought improvements.

Business didn't always get what it wanted. So dissatisfied were Chinese and British businessmen alike with the government's sanitation reforms that the colony's first, and last, official referendum took place in 1896. The vote was an attempt to secure the dominance of business interests on the new Sanitation Board that had been created in the wake of the plague, and thereby stymie government regulations. Although businessmen voted 90 percent in favor of more business representation, the government refused to accept the results. Wrote Governor William Robinson, "I believe that the Chinese, who are indifferently represented, and the Portuguese, who are not represented at all, if a plebiscite could be taken, would be in favor of a pure autocracy; the Americans need not to be counted, and the 'Britishers' with the exception of a few 'unquiet spirits' would be satisfied to let matters remain as they are."[13]

The notion that "Hong Kong people don't care about politics" has been repeated so often that it has blinded government and the business elite alike to the reality that Hong Kong people care deeply about politics. Popular political resistance has been evident in the city since the nineteenth century. Yet, from the beginning, Hong Kong Chinese business leaders have worked with the government to tamp down political disputes and undercut efforts for enhanced political participation.

An early instance of the role of the business elite in tempering political demands came in 1905–6 amid an anti-American boycott following the renewal of the Chinese Exclusion Act. This was the only legislation in U.S. history that explicitly banned immigration on ra-cial grounds. The law first passed in 1882 and was periodically re-newed until it was extended without limitation at the end of 1904.[14]

Chinese communities in China proper and throughout South-east Asia joined a boycott of American goods. The Chinese business community in Hong Kong offered only tepid support, citing pressure from British authorities. In response to a call from the Shanghai Chamber of Commerce to join the boycott, the Hong Kong Chinese Commercial Union at first promised its backing but noted that "the matter of boycott had not been discussed due to its incompatibility with the British laws."

The boycott took place in the waning days of the Qing Empire, at the end of two millennia of Chinese imperial rule. Some Hong Kong Chinese newspapers supported revolutionaries who wanted to overthrow the Qing, others backed reformers who believed consti-tutional changes could save the monarchy. Both the revolutionaries and the constitutionalists favored the boycott of American goods. Yet Governor Matthew Nathan claimed, based on his meeting with the two Chinese members of the Legislative Council, "that the 'boycott' was not wanted by any respectable merchant here."[15] Hong Kong Chinese Commercial Union chairman Fung Wah-chuen, one of the colony's most prominent Chinese businessmen, was attacked publicly through anonymous placards and privately in threatening letters. An American-trained Chinese dentist said that the public had threatened to boycott him because of his U.S. education.[16]

The movement that supported the boycott was made up of students, teachers, journalists, and revolutionary intelligentsia. It foreshadowed movements that would take place a century later, in 2003, 2014, and 2019.[17] Visiting Secretary of War (and later president) William Taft along with President Theodore Roosevelt's daughter, Alice Roosevelt, and six U.S. senators visited the colony in 1905 and met with a group of "representative Hong Kong Chinese." The resentment toward the official American delegation due to the Exclusion Law was such that chair coolies were urged to refuse to carry the group.[18] The Chinese who met the Americans pressed for reform of the anti-Chinese legislation, so as to allow for easier access to the United States by the elite. One American noted that "the merchants certainly do not care whether the coolie is excluded from America or not[,] as [they have] nothing in common with the coolie and [have] no regard for his interests."[19] Of course, coolies and other Chinese workers did care deeply about this legislation, given the significant level of Chinese immigration to the States. Summing up the anti-American boycott campaign of 1905–6, scholar Jung-fang Tsai noted that "[i]n a crisis situation the elite in the commercial union could no longer pretend to represent the consensus of the Chinese community in the colony."[20]

This pattern persisted throughout the twentieth century. In 1912, a popular and effective working-class strike took place to protest the refusal of Hong Kong Tramways to accept Chinese coins as fare payment. Chinese business gave only lukewarm support for the campaign, which was designed indirectly to support the new Chinese government.[21] In the 1920s, two lengthy strikes caused serious damage to the Hong Kong economy and prompted a severe reaction by the government. The business community firmly supported the government. Immediately after 1945, there was a series of labor disputes and agitation for greater popular participation in government. Significant protests took place in 1966 and 1967, relating both to local issues (especially corruption) and to those in mainland China.

What's as notable as the political struggles themselves is the success British colonial administrators had in making common cause with the Chinese business elite to undercut movements for political, economic, and social change.

Throughout, the British elite primarily listened to Chinese business leaders. These leaders, whether for reasons of self-preservation, self-interest, class bias, or simple ideology, did not understand—or, if they did, declined to foster—the aspirations of Hong Kongers for a greater say in the running of their colony. One of the most prominent Chinese businessmen of the mid-twentieth century was Lo Man-kam, or, as he was known in English, M.K. Lo. Lo, the son-in-law of Hong Kong's richest man, Robert Hotung, and the son of a comprador at Jardine Matheson, was a crusader for racial equality, working for decades to remove the barrier of "racial disabilities" and "promoting good fellowship within the Colony, irrespective of race, class and creed."[22] Yet M.K. Lo played a critical role in defeating the Young Plan, a postwar reform proposal that would have allowed for more democracy in Hong Kong politics.

Nobel laureate and economist Milton Friedman famously declared, "If you want to see capitalism in action, go to Hong Kong." The colony had earned a well-deserved reputation as one of the world's freest economies. It was a free port; it imposed no income tax, and it levied duties on only a handful of luxuries, such as wine, spirits, and automobiles. An aversion to government action meant compulsory education wasn't instituted until 1971; even then, just three years of primary school were required. A minimum wage was introduced only in 2009. Free-marketers embraced the tiny colony for its low taxes and lack of government regulation. The dark side of Hong Kong's well-deserved reputation as a place of anything-goes economic freedom was the systematic exclusion of the voices of most of the colony's inhabitants.

SIX

A "DYING CITY" RISES FROM THE RUINS

"This dying city."[1] That's what an American journalist, in a phrase echoed by the governor and other senior officials, called Hong Kong in the early 1950s. The despair was understandable. The city's role as an entrepôt for the China trade ended abruptly when far-reaching embargoes were imposed against the new People's Republic of China both by the United Nations and the United States. (The American one was stricter.) Even as the economy withered, the colony was overrun with refugees. More than a million people slipped into the city by sea and by land. Hungry children wandered muddy alleys. Fires ripped through wooden shantytowns, displacing tens of thousands of people in a single blaze. Diseases (tuberculosis, cholera, malaria) swept through the streets. From the ruins of war in 1945, the colony's rulers were confronting what looked like an insoluble political and humanitarian crisis.

Refugees, disease, poverty—these were the unlikely foundations on which Hong Kong's postwar prosperity was built. During the war years, the city's population had dropped by more than two thirds, to roughly five hundred thousand people.[2] After fighting stopped in August 1945, many of those who had left began filtering back across the border from China's neighboring Guangdong Province; the colony's population tripled immediately after the war, as a million people returned home. They found a city in ruins. The colony had been bombed by American planes. Postwar looting caused even more damage. A desperate need for fuel for heating and cooking meant that little was safe. The Royal Hong Kong Yacht Club's new clubhouse on Kellett Island had opened in 1940. It had survived the war intact, but the peace proved ruinous. In the two weeks between the Japanese surrender on August 15, 1945, and the reoccupation of Hong Kong by British forces at the end of the month, the yacht club was stripped. Wooden flooring and furniture were used for firewood. The grand mansion of Paul Chater, an Armenian Jew who grew up in Calcutta and had been responsible for the Central reclamation on which the city's business district sat, suffered a similar fate; his extensive art collection was plundered.

Seventy percent of the city's European-style buildings were destroyed.[3] Foraging for fuel in resource-poor Hong Kong continued until supplies of coal arrived. The electricity company China Light and Power burned trees uprooted from hillsides to keep its boilers going and its electricity turbines spinning. Lawrence Kadoorie, whose family owned China Light, recalled the "extraordinary sight" of the massive boiler being fueled by as many as four hundred tons of firewood a day. "A large number of women (some with babies tied to their backs) and a few men are busy continuously pushing this wood into the boiler."[4]

The physical scars remained for several years. Governor Alexander Grantham, who took up his post in 1947, remembers presiding over the first University of Hong Kong graduation ceremony on a chilly winter day at the end of that year in a roofless Grand Hall. During the war, parts of the campus had been excavated following unfounded rumors that the school sat atop coal deposits.

Hong Kong, initially under military administration, found its footing with remarkable speed. By 1948, *Collier's* magazine proclaimed that the city was back.

Hong Kong is the boom town of the Orient today, the only city in the Far East approaching the bright-light bustle of the "good old pre-war days," and its British stability has lured thousands of wealthy Chinese families as well as thousands of hungry coolies from what the colonials here for a century have been calling "the troubles in China." That stability has also quieted, at least temporarily, Chinese demands for the return of Hong Kong to China. As long as the civil war rages and economic chaos impends, most Chinese seem to think the Union Jack looks all right over the City of Refuge.[5]

The Communist victory in China came the next year, with the proclamation of the People's Republic of China on October 1, 1949, by Mao Zedong, a charismatic landowner's son who had become a hardened revolutionary. The CCP's onetime ragtag army of peasants and urban intellectuals had endured repeated pummeling by their Nationalist (KMT) rivals dating back to the 1920s, survived the Japanese invasion and subsequent occupation of China in 1937 before prevailing in the bitter Civil War that started again after Japan's 1945 defeat. The Chinese Communist victory prompted yet more refugees to flee to Hong Kong, notably Shanghai's commercial and financial elite.

Mao's dispatch of Chinese troops to fight alongside Kim Il-sung's North Koreans in 1950 provoked a U.S. embargo followed by one imposed by the United Nations. The tougher American embargo was in turn adopted by many U.S. allies. The embargoes further walled China off from the world and caused new problems for Hong Kong, reducing economic contacts because of strict U.S. prohibitions on trading with Communist Chinese entities. The colony was in the crosshairs; Grantham had to defend it against charges that it was helping the Communist Chinese get around economic sanctions. Hong Kong exported dried ducks to the United States; many were hatched in the city from eggs that had been laid in China. "Were the ducks from these eggs Communist ducks or true-blue British ducks?" Grantham asked. After "voluminous correspondence" with

Americans, a system to certify Hong Kong–born ducks was set up. "We could export our ducks."[6]

In the decade after the 1949 Communist takeover of the mainland, Hong Kong's population doubled again. By the time the first census in three decades took place in 1960, the population had reached three million. Few places have confronted a human crisis of this size. In the 1950s, nine hundred thousand people lived in slums or shantytowns.[7] Initially, officials thought that many of these inhabitants would return to China. As the Communist grip tightened, that expectation vanished. The border with China was shut in 1951. Immigrants sneaked across the short land border the colony shared with neighboring Shenzhen. More commonly, they came by water, swimming, often clinging to inner tubes or pieces of wood, or hidden in boats. To take one example out of the estimated 1.5 million refugees during the 1945–60 period, Jimmy Lai, famous later as media entrepreneur and pro-democracy advocate, came hidden in the bottom of a sampan at the age of twelve. As political campaigns and famine both worsened, people escaped from China however they could. The tide of humanity swelled again in the early 1960s as famine ate at the country.

Numerous fires, most commonly the result of cooking accidents among the flammable huts, destroyed squatters' camps; more than fifty thousand people were burned out in a 1953 Christmas fire alone. Malaria was endemic. Typhoid and cholera were commonplace. So, too, was tuberculosis: in 1959, sixty thousand people, or 2 percent of the population, had active cases.[8] The British military ran soup kitchens where thousands of hungry refugees patiently lined up to receive a bowl of rice gruel. With no minimum wage and no compulsory education, Hong Kong was, as one book title termed it, a "capitalist paradise" filled with three million hardworking, often desperate people.[9] If one set aside the number of soldiers and policemen who helped keep order, Chinese made up all but about twenty-five thousand of those nearly three million.

Reading accounts written in the 1950s by Grantham and other officials, I am struck by the anxiety of the British colonial officials, the sense that their colony was being overrun by hordes of Chinese refugees. The dispatches of Grantham, who administered the colony from 1947 to 1957, reflect a mixture of pleading, desperation, fear, and belief in the power of free enterprise to set matters straight. The pages of official colonial dispatches are packed with details of disease, overcrowding, hunger, and poverty and express the worries of those struggling to keep the colony functioning. A low-level proxy civil war between Communist and Nationalist forces fought among the refugees added to the strain felt by the colony's British rulers. Riots between Communists and Nationalists in 1956 saw sixty dead, mostly at the hands of the police.

It was Hong Kong's brilliance to turn "the problem of people," as colonial officials termed the refugee challenge, into a source of prosperity. Looking back, one finds it hard to resist the temptation to see Hong Kong's success as an inevitable, almost preordained, part of a wave of postwar growth in East Asia. Japan and the Four Tigers (or Four Dragons), a group that included Singapore, South Korea, and Taiwan, in addition to Hong Kong, pioneered a new growth model. But the rise of Asian economies, which many people considered an economic miracle, was largely invisible at the time. It felt to many of those living through it like a simple struggle for survival.

The refugees—their labor, their capital, their technical know-how, and their international networks—provided the engine for Hong Kong's economic acceleration. Though refugees were seen as carriers of diseases and disorder, they were in fact Hong Kong's salvation. The commercial collapse of Shanghai following the Communist takeover in 1949 proved pivotal for the development of modern Hong Kong. As Shanghai's business elite pondered where to move, they considered locations ranging from Brazil to Mauritius. China Light and Power's Lawrence Kadoorie wooed Shanghainese textile tycoons and other factory owners with the promise of ample electricity at a time when the rest of Asia suffered power shortages. Many took him up on the offer. Textile machinery that had been ordered from abroad was diverted on the high seas from a dying Shanghai to a newly important Hong Kong, jump-starting textile manufacturing and laying the groundwork for Hong Kong to become one of the world's largest exporters a decade later.

Members of a modern Chinese urban elite that was created during the Republican period (1912–49), following the collapse of the final Chinese dynasty, flowed to Hong Kong: not just men, but also increasingly powerful and well-educated women. Communist Chinese propaganda disparages the period from the fall of the Qing dynasty in 1911 until the establishment of the People's Republic in 1949 as a time of incessant conflict. This is at best a half-truth. The Republican period was a time of urbanization and modernization, one that saw the disappearance of the traditional men's braided queue hairstyle, the establishment of schools for women, the opening of department stores, and the electrification of cities.

The open, modern world of the Republican period was violently extinguished in Mao's Communist China, but it flourished in Hong Kong. The colony's neon signs and bright shop windows, its noisy factories and crowded port, stood in sharp contrast to dark and dour Maoist China just across the border. Hong Kong was a haven, protected by British rule of law and run by competent and largely hands-off administrators. Despite the snobbishness and racism of Hong Kong's elites, there was nonetheless ample room for the majority-Chinese population to thrive.

Shanghainese entrepreneurs who came to the colony after 1945, and in the wake of the 1949 Communist revolution on the mainland, brought a new self-confidence to Hong Kong's Chinese business community. Shanghai had been one of the world's most cosmopolitan cities, and many of its Chinese residents had occupied positions of prominence. The Shanghai International Settlement functioned as a sort of free territory; Chinese law did not apply. But Shanghai was not a colony. It was, unusually, or perhaps even uniquely in colonial Asia, both powerful and multinational. The Settlement's affairs were run by an elected municipal council that had the power of taxation. During the 1930s, Chinese representatives occupied more than one-third of the seats on the council. Unlike in Hong Kong—where a governor appointed by the British monarch and his administrative officers ran the colony and where the unelected appointees to the Legislative Council acted as only the most modest check on executive powers—the Shanghai Municipal Council ran the Settlement. It owned the electricity company, waterworks, and tramways and controlled the fire service, police force, and even militia.

The colonial cringe (the deference and feeling of inferiority) that characterized the Cantonese community was alien to the prominent Shanghainese who moved to Hong Kong.[10] The Shanghainese were more confident than their local Cantonese counterparts. One Shanghainese transplant later remembered, "Hong Kong was still very colonial, with the government and foreign firms high on top. Local people were not even welcome in the HSBC. The Bank was like a Chinese magistrate's court, which locals would avoid. And the Bank was not interested in their deposits. When we first arrived, we were not used to this environment."[11] Shanghainese entrepreneurs had modern equipment, overseas educations, and international sales networks. Textile industrialist Y.C. Wang was one of those whom Lawrence Kadoorie lured to Hong Kong with a promise of ample electricity. Wang set up the Nanyang Cotton Mill in 1947, and it started operations in 1948 with fifteen thousand spindles.[12] The uprooting of factories from Shanghai prompted some companies to start in Hong Kong with new equipment, forcing an upgrading of the industry.

The Shanghainese and the Cantonese often went their own ways. Many Cantonese were suspicious of the pushy, no-nonsense Shanghainese style. Even today there is tension between the Shanghainese and Cantonese. A strong Shanghainese network, bolstered by clan associations and restaurants, nurtures a sense of identity that has spanned generations.

The combination of Shanghainese and Hong Kong entrepreneurs, willing workers, ample supplies of electricity and water, and a superb port with connections to the rest of the world gave Hong Kong a head start in economic growth over its East Asian rivals. The protection of the colonial umbrella also helped. Korea and Taiwan were both distracted by ongoing civil wars. Singapore was in the midst of a prolonged struggle for independence, first from Britain and then from Malaysia, which led to it becoming a separate nation in 1965.

The decades after World War II saw Hong Kong's transformation from a middle-ranking trading port into one of the world's largest exporters and changed how the United States and the world thought of Asia. As Britain's imperial strength waned, the United States took on the role of Hong Kong's military protector, the Pacific Fleet acting as guarantor of the postwar Pax Americana. Hong Kong became an important part of the Cold War battleground. After America imposed a total embargo on trade with China in 1950, the United States used Hong Kong, and the large consulate it built up there—"a larger American staff than any of their consulates anywhere else in the world," in Grantham's words—from which to watch China. For Americans, wrote Grantham, Hong Kong "was ideally situated as a base from which to conduct anti-Communist activities, such as propaganda, espionage, and even more dubious operations."[13]

In 1957, U.S. president Dwight Eisenhower secretly pledged to protect Hong Kong in case of a Chinese attack. It was only a few years since the airlift that saved West Berlin. Grantham gave a lecture tour in America—the first time a governor had done so—to enlist American support for a place that he said was becoming the Berlin of Asia, a city that offered a beacon of freedom in a sea of communism.[14] This was in the wake of Joseph McCarthy's witch hunts of the early 1950s, during which suspicion of alleged Communist infiltration in the United States government raised the question "Who lost China?" The anticommunist obsession poisoned American life and cost many officials their careers, including many who knew China best.

Grantham defended Hong Kong against charges that it was aiding Communist China before audiences as diverse as the Council on Foreign Relations and the nationwide *Longines Chronoscope* program that ran on the CBS television network. *Longines* host Larry LeSueur started the program by noting, "Most of us have become familiar with the name Hong Kong, if not with that British Crown colony itself, because of the Korean War, and those charges that the island of Hong Kong was furnishing Communist China with the sinews of war while British and American troops were fighting the Chinese Communists on the other side, in Korea." Hong Kong was sandwiched between the menacing "cold hostility" of China, as

Grantham termed it, and a West that was unsure of where the colony's loyalties lay.

Hong Kong had economic as well as military importance in the Cold War struggle between communism and capitalism. The colony during the 1950s and '60s blossomed into a globally significant economy, with textile exports particularly prominent, and an exemplar of what free markets could accomplish. This was even more remarkable in a colony that was straining under a refugee crisis. It was an era in which Asia's population growth seemed destined to overwhelm economic growth, as Swedish Nobel Prize–winning economist Gunnar Myrdal detailed in his influential three-volume book, *Asian Drama: An Inquiry into the Poverty of Nations.*[15] For many people throughout Asia and beyond, socialism or even communism seemed a promising alternative to capitalism. Even Hong Kong was not altogether immune from these trends. After Britain's Labour government nationalized its electricity companies, Hong Kong considered following suit. Although Hong Kong's government intervened where necessary, especially in providing housing, the economy remained more market-driven than anywhere else in the region. This light-touch colonial government approach coupled with the technical know-how and access to capital of many refugees—and the drive of most of them—produced a period of unprecedented economic growth for Hong Kong.

Freedom could be extended only so far in a colony that had no prospect of independence. After the 1941 Japanese invasion and during the three years and eight months of occupation that followed, plans had been developed to give Hong Kong more political freedom. In part, this was a British gambit to prevent Hong Kong from being turned over to the Chinese Nationalists by U.S. president Franklin Delano Roosevelt, who opposed the idea of colonies. His death in April 1945, and the subsequent recapture of Hong Kong by British forces at the end of the war in August, postponed the inevitable for another fifty-two years.

It was somewhat improbable that the British managed to recover Hong Kong at the end of World War II. Either the Nationalists (KMT) or the rival Communists (CCP) might more plausibly have taken Hong Kong—although neither did, for fear of provoking the other. After the Communists took power on the mainland in 1949, they could at any moment have seized Hong Kong. No one need have worried. China was too preoccupied with establishing political control at home. The purging of millions of businessmen and intellectuals took priority.

China made it clear that it would take Hong Kong back in 1997—earlier if need be. That implicit threat limited the colony's room for maneuver, notably when it came to political reform. But the long colonial good-bye also allowed for more than a half century in which Hong Kong could develop its own identity without thoughts of nationhood or sovereignty. While colonies were being granted independence throughout Asia, there was no prospect of that for Hong Kong. Governor Grantham summarized the challenge: "Hong Kong can never become independent. Either it remains a British colony, or it is reabsorbed into China."[16]

Grantham looked forward to an extended period of colonial rule, but one that had a definite end date: "1997 will be the fateful year, for in that year the lease of the New Territories runs out, and I could not conceive of any Chinese government of whatever complexion renewing the lease. Nor could I imagine the rump of the Colony—the island of Hong Kong and the tip of the Kowloon Peninsula—continuing to exist as a viable entity, with the great bulk of the water supplies coming from the New Territories, and the dividing line between the leased and the ceded parts running right through the new runway at Kai Tak, the airport."[17]

The great shortcoming of Grantham's rule stemmed from his condescending attitude toward the local Chinese. There had been an opening for political reform immediately after the war. As noted, under the threat that U.S. president Franklin Delano Roosevelt would block Britain from retaking Hong Kong when the war ended, plans were developed during the conflict to open up the colony to more political participation by the local Hong Kong Chinese. There was a long way to go. The British had not trusted the Chinese enough to give them weapons to help stem the Japanese invasion. The first Chinese official (as opposed to clerk) to serve in the colonial government was Paul Tsui, a resistance fighter and war hero who joined the government in 1949. Tsui was hired only because it was clear that the British needed a better understanding of what was going on in their colony if they were to avoid invasion or a revolutionary uprising in the rural New Territories. Tsui remembers going to the washroom at the government secretariat in October 1946, only to be greeted by a sign in English and Chinese stating, "Europeans only."[18]

Governor Mark Young's surrender of Hong Kong marked the first military loss of a British colony since Gen. Charles Cornwallis's capitulation to George Washington at Yorktown in 1781. Young had endured harsh captivity at the hands of the Japanese, ending up as a goatherd in Manchuria. Upon his return to Hong Kong, he put forth a far-reaching electoral reform bill that would have allowed the popular election of a powerful municipal council. Following Young's departure in 1947, Grantham and a combination of British and Chinese elites killed the bill. Grantham, in his autobiography, claimed that Hong Kong was different from other colonies "in that the Chinese—and 99 percent of the population in Hong Kong is Chinese—are, generally speaking, politically apathetic." He noted that political reform was one of the first issues pursued by the government after the war, "but with singularly little interest shown by the local populace."[19]

Grantham opined that "Hong Kong has to be, and is, content with a benevolent autocracy." His arguments were misleading. He overrode broad community support for political reform in order to see that the Young Plan was never adopted. In fact, the postwar years, beginning with the Young Plan, marked the emergence of civil society in Hong Kong. Barrister Brook Bernacchi founded the Reform Club in 1949, to push for the Young Plan, later summarizing his motivation by asking, "How can one purport to represent nearly six million people in Hong Kong when you have been elected by only 6,000 voters?" Bernacchi and former English missionary turned social crusader Elsie Tu (née Elliott) were Westerners who spoke up for the people of Hong Kong.

There were Chinese voices in support of change as well. Ma Man-fai, a member of the prominent family that founded Shanghai's

Sincere Department Store, started the United Nations Association of Hong Kong to work for self-government for the territory. Hilton Cheong-leen, born in British Guyana, cofounded another significant reform group in the 1950s, the Hong Kong Civic Association, and worked with Ma Man-fai on the United Nations Association. These were all moderate professionals, businessmen, and lawyers for the most part, and not allied with the KMT or the CCP.

A more explicitly political figure was Percy Chen. Born in Trinidad, Chen was the son of former KMT foreign minister Eugene Chen. Percy Chen followed his father back to China. (He later lived in Moscow for six years, became disenchanted with the KMT, allied himself with the Communists, and acted as an adviser to General Motors in its negotiations with the Soviet government.) All were united in wanting political and social change. Their efforts focused on education, health, and political reform. Sometimes they fought on the economic front, failing in the late 1950s and early 1960s to merge and nationalize the colony's two electricity companies. The reformers had little immediate success, but their efforts give the lie to the dominant narrative that Hong Kongers did not care about politics until near the end of the British colonial period.

The defeat of the Young Plan spelled the end of any meaningful political reform movement in Hong Kong for three decades. It would not be until Thatcher's 1982 visit to Beijing that reform reemerged as an issue. These early political initiatives never completely disappeared, although they were often stifled for the sake of stability, the need to keep the KMT-CCP conflict from spilling into Hong Kong, and to avoid the risk of antagonizing the People's Republic. Anticommunism and fear of Communist Party tactics that could be used to manipulate elections also inhibited demands for political reform.

The postwar period initially saw the colonial administration seize control of many sectors of the economy. Price controls, including rent control, were imposed immediately after the war. The last of these, on staple goods such as rice and coal, were not lifted until the mid-1950s. A salaries tax was introduced for the first time in peacetime in the late 1940s, though even today there is no tax on overall income. Dividends and capital gains, such as profits from stocks or property, are excluded from tax. Far from the caricatured vision that portrayed Hong Kong as a shining example of a laissez-faire economy, colonial administrators were pragmatic interventionists. The colonial state built public housing and a solid basic health system in order to stave off the social problems associated with some 1.5 million refugees. But for the most part, Hong Kong, almost alone in the world, continued to function under a light-touch government. The idea of a development bank was raised by business. No, came the answer. Industrialists wanted the government to provide cheap land for factories. Again, the answer was no. Hong Kong prided itself on being a free port, virtually eliminating paperwork on most imports.

In praising Hong Kong, Nobel Prize–winning economist Milton Friedman singled out Hong Kong's financial secretary John Cowperthwaite for his adherence to laissez-faire policies. Cowperthwaite, wrote Friedman just weeks before his death in late 2006,

> was so famously laissez-faire that he refused to collect economic statistics for fear this would only give government officials an excuse for more meddling. His successor, Sir Philip Haddon-Cave, coined the term "positive noninterventionism" to describe Cowperthwaite's approach. The results of his policy were remarkable. At the end of World War II, Hong Kong was a dirt-poor island with a per-capita income about one-quarter that of Britain's. By 1997, when sovereignty was transferred to China, its per-capita income was roughly equal to that of the departing colonial power, even though Britain had experienced sizable growth over the same period. That was a striking demonstration of the productivity of freedom, of what people can do when they are left free to pursue their own interests. . . . Whatever happens to Hong Kong in the future, the experience of this past 50 years will continue to instruct and encourage friends of economic freedom. And it provides a lasting model of good economic policy for others who wish to bring similar prosperity to their people.[20]

The hands-off policy was cruel in many individual instances, but Hong Kong had few alternatives in dealing with the 1.5 million refugees who had come to the city. Even the richest of places would have struggled to accommodate a sixfold increase in its population in just fifteen years. The raw capitalism worked its magic. Hong Kong's economic growth was among the highest and longest-lasting that any economy has ever shown achieved. The small colony emerged as one of the world's largest textile exporters and a major producer of everything from wigs to toys for markets around the world.

One danger of a laissez-faire policy is that it may degenerate into utter passivity. Only after Cowperthwaite retired was three years of compulsory primary school education instituted. Cowperthwaite also rejected the idea of a government-funded public transit system. The MTR subway, started after he left office, has become one of Hong Kong's biggest successes and continues to expand abroad.

The tide of refugees that engulfed postwar Hong Kong led to appalling misery. It also catalyzed a period of unprecedented economic prosperity. Grantham's embrace of the free market—"Hurray for the free market," he wrote in a visitors' book when touring Kadoorie's newest electricity station—served the colony well. Even though Grantham's neutering of calls for political change and more meaningful popular participation had long-term costs that are still being paid, Hong Kong took advantage, economically and socially, of extended colonial rule. The Chinese ensured that Hong Kong would not become independent, but the territory used the five decades remaining in its colonial lease to develop as a place unique in its commitment to free markets and free people, enjoying the benefit of the rule of law, an open society, and good government. Hong Kong was not democratic, but it was free.

SEVEN

"HORSES WILL STILL RUN, STOCKS WILL STILL SIZZLE, DANCERS WILL STILL DANCE"

Margaret Thatcher was flush from Britain's victory over Argentina's military dictatorship in the Falkland Islands when, in September 1982, she became the first serving British prime minister to visit Beijing. Her visit was prompted by the looming expiration of the ninety-nine-year lease on Hong Kong's New Territories and "the difficult question of the future of Hong Kong," as her advisers framed the visit. While Hong Kong Island and a small strip of the mainland, in Kowloon, had been ceded to Britain in perpetuity, the largest part of the colony would revert to China in 1997. Hong Kong had long depended on China for much of its water and food. The colony was militarily indefensible. If China wanted Hong Kong back, Britain would have no choice but to agree. With only fifteen years to go, banks and businesses needed clarity on what would follow. Property was at the heart of the Hong Kong economy, and many properties were financed with fifteen-year mortgages. If contracts would not be legally enforceable after June 30, 1997, the Hong Kong economy was likely to collapse.

Thatcher wanted China to be the first stop on her visit to Asia, in order to be done with it. "Communist countries are always the most strenuous," she wrote her private secretary as the trip was being planned. In the end, she went first to Japan and then flew to Peking, as the British government insisted on calling the Chinese capital. Characteristically, the resolutely anticommunist Thatcher refused the suggestion that she lay a wreath in Tiananmen Square to honor the martyrs of the country's revolutionary struggles.

Thatcher met with Premier Zhao Ziyang for two hours the afternoon she arrived from Tokyo and another two hours the following morning. That afternoon, she met the paramount Chinese leader, Deng Xiaoping. Special silver, including a statue of the Duke of Wellington, was borrowed from a reluctant Royal Navy and brought from London for a banquet at the Great Hall of the People. Ambassador Percy Cradock won Thatcher's approval to up the per-head banquet cost to 75 yuan ($40) from the proposed 50 yuan ($26), in order to serve Chinese guests delicacies such as sea slugs and shark fin.[1] Thatcher agreed to serve champagne, but the frugal prime minister nixed caviar canapés from the menu for her flight out ("No—much too expensive!")

Thatcher took care with her dress and made notes about which outfits she would wear. For her day of meetings with Zhao Ziyang and Deng Xiaoping, she wore her "fuchsia—plum stars" dress. When she hosted a banquet at the Great Hall of the People in Beijing, she wore "a brilliant scarlet dress," remembers private secretary John Coles, "not of course as a sycophantic gesture to Communist China but because she had been told that for the Chinese red signified happiness and that it would be an appropriate color to wear at a celebratory occasion."[2]

Thatcher did not believe that the Chinese Communists could successfully administer a prosperous Hong Kong. She pressed the Chinese to agree to continued British administration for several more decades. Against the advice of China experts, notably Cradock, she told Deng and Zhao that the British would be willing to return sovereignty to China but wanted British administration to continue. Deng literally spat at Thatcher's suggestion, hocking into the spittoon beside his chair. China was going to take Hong Kong back, he told Thatcher.

No, he told the woman known as the Iron Lady, China did not need British administration. China would be able to manage Hong Kong just fine. And if it didn't, so be it. For the Chinese, Hong Kong was a matter of national pride. Securing the return of Hong Kong would go a long way toward righting the wrongs of what the Chinese saw as a century of humiliation and would bolster the Communist Party's claim to legitimacy by recovering lost territory.

The next day, when Thatcher left the Great Hall of the People after lunch, she tripped and fell down a flight of stairs, ending on her hands and knees at the bottom of the steps. The clip of her humiliating fall was replayed endlessly on television in Hong Kong, where people were awaiting news of the colony's fate.

Thatcher's fall and her meetings in Beijing symbolized a dramatic reversal of historical fortunes. Britain's first envoy to China, George Macartney, had by his own account famously refused to kowtow to the Qianlong emperor during his mission to Peking in 1793. The intervening two centuries had seen Britain defeat China in the two Opium Wars and impose what the Chinese regarded as humiliating extraterritorial treaties, the terms of which included Qing cession in perpetuity of Hong Kong Island in 1841 and of the Kowloon Peninsula south of Boundary Street in 1860, as well as a ninety-nine-year lease on the New Territories in 1898. With the expiration of the New Territories lease only fifteen years away, Deng and China's other leaders were determined to erase the colonial legacy of unequal treaties embodied in British rule over Hong Kong.

Both sides knew that Britain had little negotiating leverage. China could probably take over Hong Kong without firing a shot. The threat of an armed incursion would be enough to panic the colony into submission. China, needing international help for Deng's economic development program, also needed to move cautiously.

Deng promised Thatcher that there would be no changes in Hong Kong's freedom after reunification. He was fond of catchy slogans on contentious issues like Hong Kong, telling Thatcher that "horses will still run, stocks will still sizzle, dancers will still dance."[3] Deng said that businessmen should "set their hearts at ease," a remark that promised everything but meant nothing.[4] Part of Deng's strategy was based on the misapprehension that the people of Hong Kong would welcome Chinese rule—a lie that was peddled by China's friends in the colony. China's determination to take back the colony clashed with the reality that most Hong Kongers, or their parents, had come to the colony precisely because they wanted to escape Communist China.

Deng developed what he called the "one country, two systems" plan with an eye on Taiwan. The concept was designed to woo the three remaining wayward parts of China—Hong Kong, Taiwan, and Macau—into accepting a peaceful takeover by China by promising something close to self-governance, except when it came to military and foreign affairs. Deng hoped the "high degree of autonomy" the formula offered would be so successful in Hong Kong that it would entice Taiwan to agree to reunification with the mainland (or, as Chinese prefer to call it, the "motherland").

Thatcher knew better than to think Hong Kongers would celebrate a return to China. Indeed, she harbored secret hopes that Hong Kong could gain its independence. She later said, "I would have liked to have kept the sovereignty of Hong Kong island for Britain. . . . I would have loved for them to have their independence and to be a small member of the United Nations. . . . It would have been marvelous."[5] The Chinese didn't do marvelous.

Thatcher and the people of Hong Kong shared a fear of communism and a fear of the Chinese Communist Party. Hong Kong was not a democratic colony, but it *was* a free city. This was the issue in 1982, and it remains the issue today, even if Hong Kong is now much less free than it was before mid-2020. Hong Kongers don't trust a party that has never owned up to its responsibility in killing more than forty million people through political persecution and avoidable famine. It is a party that still venerates its longtime head, Mao Zedong, the worst mass murderer in human history.

The stock market in Hong Kong was trading down. Thatcher told author Jonathan Dimbleby that "at one point Deng turned to her and rasped, 'Money is going out. You must stop it.' Thatcher replied, 'I can't. I have no powers to stop it.' [Deng responded:] 'Of course you can!' Thatcher repeated, 'I can't. I have no power suddenly to step in and stop the market operating. I have no powers under the law.' She was bewildered. 'He didn't understand. He just had no comprehension at all.'"[6]

Thatcher traveled to Hong Kong, the first serving British prime minister ever to visit the colony. While there, she met with thirty city councilors. These were the Unelected Members of the Executive and Legislative Councils, or UMELCO, the most senior body representing the Hong Kong people. Thatcher told UMELCO members that she was pushing for continuing British administration after 1997. According to official notes of the meeting, she said Chinese leaders

> had a limited understanding of what a free society was. They could grasp intellectually the concept of rule of law but they did not understand or accept that there could be fundamental rights that did not derive from the State. They thought they could run a capitalist society but they did not know what it meant. The Prime Minister had been told many times that Deng Xiaoping was "pragmatic" but his pragmatism counted for little compared with his Marxist-Leninism.[7]

In a note summarizing her meeting with UMECLO, Thatcher added a prophetic comment, one that took aim at the responsibility of the elite with whom she was meeting to tell Beijing the truth about what Hong Kongers thought: "The Prime Minister did not think that the Chinese leaders had heard the truth about what made Hong Kong a success from local personalities who had been invited to Peking." China's leaders have a habit of inviting "friends of China," who tell the leadership what they know it wants to hear, a pattern that continues today. "She had told the truth and it was not surprising that the Chinese had not accepted what she said. They had told her Singapore worked very well; she had pointed out that Singapore was an independent sovereign state."

Thatcher was correct when she said that the "real difficulty" was "to get the Chinese to understand that Hong Kong would not have become what it was today without British administration." The problem was, and it continued to be, as Thatcher said, that "Chinese leaders do not begin to understand the nature of a free society." Her faith in British concepts of freedom and rule of law were unshakeable. But colonialism—or what Thatcher euphemistically called "British administration"—was far more problematic than she ever admitted.

Thatcher's insight that China's leaders had no concept of what made Hong Kong successful, and that they were being misled by visitors from the colony, was prescient. She later wrote in her memoirs that, with talks deadlocked four months after her meeting with Deng, she privately advocated self-government for the territory. "I proposed that in the absence of progress in the talks we should now develop the democratic structure in Hong Kong as though it were our aim to achieve independence or self-government within a short period," she says. "We might also consider using referenda as an accepted institution there." She later abandoned the idea, after it failed to win the support of ministers and officials, and reluctantly conceded that Britain would have "no link of authority or accountability" with Hong Kong after 1997. She also pressed for more democratic participation during a visit to Beijing to sign the Joint Declaration in December 1984, but she received a cool response from premier Zhao Ziyang.[8]

Thatcher and her team may have gotten the best deal China would have offered. Britain had no leverage, and the "one country, two systems" formula offered some hope that Hong Kong would be able to preserve a measure of autonomy. Yet Britain kowtowed to China's insistence that the Hong Kong people not be involved in any negotiations. The secrecy around the talks was unnecessary, indefensible, and, in the end, counterproductive. Looking back, one sees this curious omission as summing up the way in which the British regarded the Hong Kong people as somehow unworthy of even knowing about negotiations that were to decide their fate. Settling the future of Hong Kong was the reason for Thatcher's 1982 visit to Beijing and Hong Kong. Yet the issue was so sensitive that the government's official 1982 yearbook never mentioned the subject. Instead, the book showed bland photos of Thatcher visiting an MTR station and a housing estate. The colony's future went undiscussed.

EIGHT

MASSACRE IN TIANANMEN

"TODAY'S CHINA IS TOMORROW'S HONG KONG"

The death of a leader has a special potency in authoritarian regimes. Death is a time for public mourning and for an outpouring of emotion and grievance that would not normally be tolerated. So it was fitting that the death of a former Communist Party leader provided the catalyst for the most extended defiance of the country's leaders since the founding of the People's Republic in 1949.

Until two years before his death in April 1989, Hu Yaobang had been the Chinese Communist Party's general secretary. His was the top position in China's hybrid party-government structure, and certainly more important than the top government job of president. Conservatives had opposed Hu's modest moves toward political and economic openness and used the excuse of student protests to remove him from office in early 1987. Compelled to issue a humiliating self-criticism and stripped of political power, he became a symbol of integrity within a party that seemed to have lost its way. At his funeral, his widow told Deng Xiaoping that her husband's death was "all because of you people."[1] Hu's passing reminded people of how badly the party had treated one of its true revolutionary leaders and brought a line of mourners that stretched for ten miles through the streets of Beijing.

What began as a funeral procession on April 15 soon became a protest camp in the vast Tiananmen Square, a rallying point for grievances ranging from the continuing behind-the-scenes influence of party elders, to favored treatment for their "princeling" children, to corruption and inflation. Widespread frustration and unhappiness prompted calls for democracy that unnerved the leadership. Demonstrations broke out throughout the country. About half the journalists at the flagship Communist Party newspaper *People's Daily* supported the protesters, running a series of articles in favor of the students and putting out an unauthorized extra edition of the paper that took the students' side. The paper—and, indeed, the Communist Party itself—was splitting. Throughout the country, there were calls for democracy, but also demands to end corruption and to do something about the inflation that had resulted from the economic reforms initiated during the previous decade.

The protests were both an unprecedented political challenge and a very public embarrassment for China's leaders. "New China," the People's Republic, had been founded forty years earlier, but Mao Zedong had dominated the early years. Even in 1989, thirteen years after his death, Mao's shadow still loomed, and it was not clear what path the country would choose. Would Deng's reform and opening prevail, or would those pushing orthodox Communist policies win the day?

Soviet party leader Mikhail Gorbachev arrived in Beijing in May, the first visit by a Soviet leader since the bitter split between the two countries in the 1950s. His welcoming ceremony at the Great Hall of the People on the edge of Tiananmen Square had to be canceled because of the crowds. Beijing also hosted a meeting of the Asian Development Bank as the Tiananmen demonstrations continued. What should have been a sort of coming-out party, where Beijing welcomed, and was welcomed into, the Western-dominated world of development finance, proved a humiliation for a regime used to wielding total control when hosting international events and foreign visitors.

Shortly after five o'clock on the morning of May 19, reformist premier Zhao Ziyang went to meet students in Tiananmen Square. Zhao begged the students to stop a hunger strike they had started a week earlier. It was Zhao's last public appearance. He was purged and placed under house arrest until his death in 2005. Zhao's replacement as premier was hard-liner Li Peng, and the crackdown was backed by paramount leader Deng Xiaoping, whose official position in 1989 was chairman of the Central Military Commission. Two days later in Hong Kong, in the midst of a typhoon, fifty thousand people marched in the streets in support of the students. The following Sunday, May 28, more than one million people, perhaps as many as 1.5 million, surged into the colony's streets.[2] Community support was strong, even among the leftist, pro-Beijing media. The colony had never seen anything like this public, and very political, display.

The following Saturday night, June 3, and into Sunday, June 4, the People's Liberation Army invaded—there is really no other word to describe it—Tiananmen Square. CNN, the BBC and other broadcast media were there. Satellite television was relatively young, and this was the first time that an event of this sort, certainly the first time that a Communist-orchestrated massacre, was broadcast almost as it was happening.

We will never know how many people died in the capital. Estimates generally range from several hundred to more than a thousand. Two points are perhaps more important than the numbers. First, the calculated brutality of the crackdown showed Chinese people just how far the Communist Party would go to keep its grip on power. The very public display of state violence in the heart of the capital was a warning to the country from the party: Do not cross us. The second, and related, point is that the killings were almost certainly unnecessary. The viciousness of the government response reflected a power struggle within the leadership. Premier Li Peng was consolidating his power.

Hong Kongers had been watching events in the capital nervously. With the handover looming in just eight years' time, the city's fate was bound to China's as never before. The city was in a state of collective mourning. China went into a kind of hibernation. A return to

Maoist-era policies, where political correctness was more important than economic development, seemed plausible.

The Tiananmen Square Massacre was as traumatic an event for the Chinese as the September 11, 2001, attacks on New York City and Washington later would be for Americans. In the case of Tiananmen, however, it was as if the government were the terrorists, the government the enemy attackers. The massacre was launched by the government against the Chinese people, and the government won. Not only did the party win, but it arrested and jailed and expelled the losers.

The Tiananmen killings were not a glorious victory over enemies or terrorists. The party first defended the event, sometimes half-heartedly and sometimes vigorously, as necessary to prevent a counterrevolutionary uprising. As years passed, Beijing's strategy shifted: at first it issued defensive denials and justifications; later, it simply scrubbed away the event. The bloodied streets of Beijing represented a terrible stain on the party, one that needed to be hidden, talked about only in secret. The government has lied and covered it up to this day. No mention of the Tiananmen killings is allowed on social media or the internet in mainland China, let alone in books, magazines, or newspapers available to Chinese citizens. References that would make sense only to those who already know about the killings—for example, the combination of "six" and "four" (denoting the sixth month and the fourth day, or June 4)—are banned in China, quickly deleted from social media.

The party has largely succeeded and, a generation later, has so expunged what occurred from the official historical memory that many or most people under the age of thirty know nothing about the massacre. Young Chinese who study abroad and discover what happened often express feelings of shock, surprise, and anger when they learn about the Tiananmen killings. Chris Patten, who was the colony's last governor, tells of his wife Lavender's visit to a British private school. She met mainland Chinese students who knew of Tiananmen as the site of the Monument to the People's Heroes, a towering obelisk commemorating martyrs in the revolutionary struggle and a symbol of national pride. They were bewildered and stunned when they learned the truth of the June 4, 1989, killings around the square and what "Tiananmen" means to people outside mainland China.

Yet everyone in Hong Kong knows about the Tiananmen killings. As I saw on the way home from the June 4 vigil in 2019, it's common for a schoolboy to learn his history by watching the "Tank Man" video. Until the 2020 crackdown, tens of thousands would join annual commemorations of the massacre. The word "Tiananmen" in Hong Kong and outside mainland China is shorthand for the violence that the Chinese Communist Party is prepared to inflict to keep its hold on power.

The Tiananmen Square Massacre came little more than a decade after the death of Mao and the arrest of the Gang of Four in 1976. Mao's China had wasted three decades trying to implement his terrible policies. From 1958 to 1962 came the Great Leap Forward, designed to accelerate the transition from a rural peasant economy to a Communist one. This half-baked scheme to catch up with England and the United States saw people melting down useful metal objects (tools, cooking pots, doors) to make useless scrap metal in primitive backyard smelters. We often talk about Potemkin villages, a historical misnomer given the reality of the development that Grigory Potemkin spurred in southern Russia. We should be talking about Maoist villages instead, with transplanted rice shoots and newly built agricultural hamlets masking the reality of the worst man-made famine in human history. Somewhere between thirty million and forty-five million died as a result of the hunger that followed the ironically named Great Leap Forward. Mao knew that people were starving, yet he insisted that officials forcibly requisition one-third of the grain for cities and, incredibly, even for export. This was at a time when fewer than one-sixth of Chinese lived in cities.

Those who tried to challenge Mao's disastrous stewardship found themselves caught up in his murderous political campaigns. Defense Minister Peng Dehuai, a revolutionary from a peasant family, was one of the few who stood up. He was angrily dismissed by Mao, denounced as "bourgeois," and imprisoned, tortured, and beaten. His treatment ensured that others would not dare oppose Mao. Historian Frank Dikötter, one of a handful of researchers who has consulted original archival records, estimates that of the forty-five million people who died as a result of the Great Leap Forward, at least 2.5 million people were beaten or tortured to death, while between one million and three million committed suicide. The Great Leap forward spilled over into Hong Kong. Although the border was closed to most normal traffic, as many as eighty thousand refugees in a single month illegally crossed into the colony in 1962.[3]

The tragedy of the Great Leap Forward was followed a few years later by the deliberate chaos of the Cultural Revolution. This was Mao's attempt to keep the revolutionary spirit alive a quarter century after the founding of the People's Republic. The decade-long campaign, from 1966 to 1976, featured student Red Guards who, by most accounts, killed at least one million people.

Mao is without a doubt one of the great monsters of history. Though he unified a fractious country, he killed more of his own country's people than anyone in history. Yet his massive portrait still hangs above the arch on Tiananmen Square, below the proscenium where he proclaimed the founding of the People's Republic of China on October 1, 1949, and later watched uniformed Red Guard students parade during the Cultural Revolution. Mao's portrait is on all but the smallest denomination of Chinese currency. One Chinese government document that has circulated unofficially blames Mao for eighty million deaths of his own people after coming to power—Stalin and Hitler *together* were responsible for roughly the same number of deaths—yet there's been no serious attempt to come to grips with Mao's legacy.

Deng Xiaoping implied that Mao was 70 percent right and 30 percent wrong. This circumlocution represents the sum total of the Chinese government's attempts to account for tens of millions of needless and often excruciatingly painful deaths.[4] The few attempts to critically assess his legacy have been small-scale and low-key. There are no museums to the victims of the Great Leap Forward or the Cultural Revolution on the mainland, no documentaries featuring relatives of those who died or scholars who question Mao's legacy. Imagine if the Germans continued to celebrate Hitler as an avuncular vegetarian who restored German pride and national sovereignty, with his image displayed as a talismanic lucky charm by taxi drivers and his portrait hung on the front of the newly restored Reichstag. Such is the People's Republic's treatment of Mao.

Hong Kongers have seen the political violence inflicted by the Chinese Communist Party. They and their relatives, neighbors, and friends have suffered and sought refuge in Hong Kong. They have little or no say in Hong Kong's political system, so it is no surprise that many of them would claim—at least when speaking to those in positions of authority (teachers, policemen, bosses, foreigners)—that they do not care about politics. It's not that they don't care, but they have had to pretend that they don't. Being politically engaged in China over the past one hundred years has been dangerous.

The Tiananmen killings came almost exactly halfway between Thatcher's 1982 visit to Beijing, when she was told that the Chinese would take the colony back in 1997, and the handover date itself. A colony that had cheered China's opening under Hu Yaobang and Zhao Ziyang now watched on satellite televisions as a regime murdered its own citizens, killing students from its top universities and others in the heart of the capital.

After the massacre, a shattered Hong Kong tried to pick up the pieces. "Blood Must Be Paid with Blood," read the banners draped across the Bank of China building.[5] Rather than repaying blood with blood, many people chose to turn the other cheek by leaving. Among those who fled was the head of the news agency Xinhua Hong Kong, Xu Jaitun, Beijing's top representative in the colony.

Xu had arrived in Hong Kong in 1983, shortly after Margaret Thatcher's first trip to Beijing and the year before her second, when she signed the Sino-British Joint Declaration, which laid out the terms of the handover. Xu's tenure in Hong Kong also encompassed the start of negotiations on the Basic Law, the mini-constitution that would underpin Hong Kong's status as a region that would manage its own affairs with a "high degree of autonomy." He was a senior party member, for a time serving on the Communist Party's Central Committee. His appointment was an important one, as he was charged with softening up Hong Kong for the 1997 handover. After the Tiananmen massacre, however, he fled to the United States, where he was granted political asylum and became the highest-level Communist Chinese defector in history. His defection humiliated Beijing.

Fueling Communist fears that Hong Kong could not be trusted was the colony's role in smuggling dissidents out of China. The CIA, along with British and French intelligence agencies, helped more than four hundred Chinese escape via Hong Kong in "Operation Yellow Bird." Once these Chinese dissidents reached Hong Kong, the clandestine operation helped them secure political asylum, largely in the United States and France. Having begun in June 1989, the operation did not end until shortly before the 1997 handover. Yellow Bird confirmed Chinese suspicion that Hong Kong was a base of subversion against the mainland.[6]

Even before the Tiananmen killings, emigration had been increasing in the wake of the 1984 Sino-British agreement. In 1987, thirty thousand people emigrated from Hong Kong. In 1988, the number rose to forty-five thousand. The river became a torrent after Tiananmen. Emigration boomed as families chose to leave before the Communists arrived—but most could not go to Britain.

Since the 1960s, Hong Kongers had been penalized by Britain's racist policies, which were designed to slow the flow of immigrants from former colonies. Those immigrants lost easy access to citizenship and suffered increasing restrictions on their ability to live and work in Britain. In 1981, they were no longer automatically allowed residence in the United Kingdom.[7] Restrictions were tightened further around the time Thatcher went to Beijing, following the publication of a British government study on immigration entitled *Who Do We Think We Are?*

In 1985, Britain established a special category called British National (Overseas), an unsatisfactory, second-class hybrid that provided passports to about five million Hong Kongers, but no right to live in Britain. The People's Republic did not recognize any of these distinctions or any of the British nationality schemes, as that would have meant recognizing the so-called unequal treaties from the nineteenth century. The Chinese would not, for example, allow

BN(O) passport holders to obtain help from British diplomats if they ran into trouble in China.

The June 4 Tiananmen killings threw this policy into crisis. To prevent a brain drain, a new scheme was developed that allowed fifty thousand key people in the colony, and all their family members, to obtain British citizenship. Several hundred thousand people emigrated from Hong Kong in the years after 1989. When I arrived in 1992, emigration was still a hot topic. Hong Kong officials worried that rival city-state Singapore was picking up Hong Kong talent. Vancouver became a favored destination, and the city's Richmond district became a Little Hong Kong known as Hongcouver. Emigrating was not a decision taken lightly. Children had to be started in new schools, in a new country, and often a new language. The phenomenon of the "astronauts" developed—fathers who would shuttle back and forth between their relatively higher-paying jobs in Hong Kong and their families in Vancouver or Toronto or Sydney or Auckland.

The Chinese hated this demonstration of fear at their impending takeover. They had told themselves that the Hong Kong "compatriots" would welcome a return to the motherland after a century and a half of British colonial rule. Hundreds of thousands of people leaving told them, and the rest of the world, otherwise.

Ironically, after all the struggles over nationality, Britain eventually, three decades later, adopted a welcoming attitude. After the National Security Law was passed in 2020, Britain removed a six-month limit on visa-free stays for Hong Kong BN(O) passport holders. On July 1, 2020, the day the National Security Law went into effect, Britain announced that, starting on January 1, 2021, all Hong Kong BN(O) holders would be eligible to enter Britain and, after five years, could apply for citizenship.[8] The Chinese reacted with rage. Perhaps they should have reflected on what they had done that made people want to leave.

❧

"Today's China Is Tomorrow's Hong Kong," proclaimed a banner Hong Kong students carried on the eve of the Tiananmen massacre.[9] The killings derailed the so-called through train, the plans for a seamless transition to Chinese rule. A sullen city waited for Beijing's arrival. Those who remained were determined to use these last few years to try to establish democratic norms. They wanted to ensure that the city would at least remain free, even if it was not democratic. This meant, above all, creating a more representative government. Hong Kongers were to get their chance, thanks to a controversial trip to Beijing by British prime minister John Major the next year and a Chinese political miscalculation that was to have historic ramifications.

NINE

"I HAVE TO LIVE IN THE REAL WORLD"

In September 1991, British prime minister John Major became the first Western leader to visit China since the 1989 Tiananmen killings. Though memories of the bloodshed were fresh, Major was determined to do the right thing by Hong Kong and get the best deal he could for its people. "It would have been safer politically not to have gone but I knew we would have to do business with China over Hong Kong and I judged that an early visit would help me do so," he reflected later. Major hoped to stabilize relations with China and smooth the road for a comfortable and undramatic transfer of power from Britain to China. "I have to live in the real world," he said at the time of the trip. "It would not be proper to sit back and strike attitudes and let Hong Kong pay the price."

John Major was a pragmatist. Where Thatcher was ideological, Major was accommodating. He had a core of decency and concern for the people of Hong Kong—though it did not extend to letting them live in Britain. He wanted Britain to leave with some sense of honor. Looking at the flawed history of colonialism, it is easy to dismiss these sorts of concerns as meaningless platitudes, but in the case of Major, Chris Patten, and many others in the British foreign policy establishment, they were genuinely felt. All these men and women knew that in the space of little more than a generation, Hong Kong people—under British administration—had transformed an impoverished, war-ravaged port city whose population had been doubled with a flood tide of refugees into one of those rare colonies that had grown as prosperous as its colonizer. One can debate the pros and cons of colonialism—and the original sin, the First Opium War, on which Hong Kong was founded cannot be ignored—but it is apparent that there was a deep reservoir of admiration among the British foreign policy establishment for what the Hong Kong people had accomplished. In another world, Hong Kong might have gained its independence. Instead, a free and prosperous people was being turned over to a Communist country.

On Major's trip to Beijing, the Chinese leadership overplayed their hand, treating him badly despite the political heat he was taking for the visit. This prompted him to lose confidence in the penultimate governor of Hong Kong, David Wilson, who would depart a few months later at the end of his term. The prime minister knew that he needed to minimize the influence of the old China hands. A quirky election result gave him the opportunity to appoint one of his closest allies, Christopher Patten, the suddenly unemployed former Member of Parliament for the spa town of Bath, as the last governor of Hong Kong. Patten pursued a democratic agenda further and faster than almost anyone had thought possible. The Chinese Communist Party's desire for a short-term tactical advantage over Britain and Major had backfired with historic consequences. Anyone who claims that the Chinese tend to favor a patient, reasoned negotiating and governing strategy must take account of this historic failure of China to ensure a smooth handover but one that fundamentally strengthened democracy in Hong Kong.

The Chinese tendency to sacrifice its long-term interests for short-term victories was prominently displayed after Tiananmen. It was not only the British, with their complicated history of conquest and colonialism, who found they were dealing with prickly and aggressive leaders in Beijing. The imminent handover of Hong Kong took on new poignancy in the wake of the Tiananmen killings, and no less a figure than Richard Nixon personally appealed to Deng Xiaoping about Hong Kong. Writing to the Chinese leader in April 1990, less than a year after the massacre in Beijing, the former president restated his belief "that a nation's policy must not be affected by soft-headed friendship. But only by hard-headed reality." In the five-page letter, Nixon wrote that "The views I express here have nothing to do with ideology. I am a capitalist. You are a Communist. Neither of us is going to change the other." Nixon said that the two countries "simply are not going to agree on what happened and why it happened on June 4 and thereafter."

Nixon had met Deng the previous October, on a private visit to Beijing. At that time, Deng told him that "the U.S. was involved too deeply in the turmoil and counterrevolutionary rebellion that occurred in Beijing not long ago . . . China was the real victim, and it is unjust to reprove China for it." Deng told Nixon that "it is up to the U.S. to take the initiative. The U.S. is capable of taking some initial steps."

In his letter, Nixon argued that the two sides must put differences aside: "It would be completely below our dignity to act like a couple of banana republics and bicker about who should apologize, who should 'untie the knot,' who goes first in repairing our relationship." He noted that China felt that its steps "have not been adequately appreciated particularly in the American media and in our Congress." He stressed that President George Bush "feels that he has gone the extra mile" without an adequate Chinese response. "What is particularly important for you to recognize is that he has taken terrible political heat from both Republicans as well as Democrats in the Congress for not taking what they believe should be a harder line toward the PRC." Bush had resisted the pressure to impose sanctions, but he might not be able to do so indefinitely, warned the former president.

Nixon counseled Deng to find a way to allow dissident physicist Fang Lizhi, who had sought refuge at the U.S. embassy in Beijing in the aftermath of the killings and remained there until the following June, to leave China. Fang, noted Nixon, "does far more harm in China than if he were outside. If he were released, he would make all of the [Western] talk shows and be hailed as a hero and thereafter he would no longer command a significant audience." Nixon said that China's refusal to let him leave the country "makes no sense at all . . . I think that such stubbornness is just plain stupid, which mystifies me because whatever one thinks of the Chinese people, they are not stupid." Nixon also advised amnesty for peaceful protesters.

Nixon then brought up Hong Kong: "Turning to another issue— Are there measures you might undertake, acknowledging British and Hong Kong suggestions, to allay fears about Hong Kong's future after 1997? Obviously Hong Kong's future is not a direct issue between our two countries, but Congress and [the American] people are concerned about Hong Kong's economic future. Some Chinese statements recently have heightened anxiety about its prospects, and it is important to try to understand and alleviate these concerns." Nixon concluded by asking Deng to make a "big play" to improve Sino-U.S. relations. In a singularly inappropriate—or deliberately provocative—metaphor, Nixon said that Deng was "the only one who has the prestige and the power to crack a few heads together and to get things moving on the right track again."[1]

Major, too, had some experience in negotiating with the Chinese, though it could not begin to match the depth or duration of Nixon's. Writing almost a decade later in his memoirs, Major struck an apologetic note as he described his first meeting with a Chinese official in the wake of Tiananmen and of the need to lie to the general public about why the encounter was going ahead. Before taking over as prime minister, Major was foreign secretary, a position he assumed in July 1989. He met his Chinese counterpart, Qian Qichen, shortly after that; this was the first official contact between Britain and China since the Tiananmen killings, when protesters were, as Major wrote, "mown down or crushed beneath the wheels of Chinese army tanks." The events had, as Major noted, shocked the world, "but in particular the vulnerable inhabitants of Hong Kong, who were due to see their territory revert to Chinese sovereignty on 1 July 1997."

Major commented that Thatcher had negotiated from "a position of hopeless weakness." As he saw it, the only issue was whether the handover would take place with an agreement or without one. "Before Tiananmen, it was possible to be optimistic. After it, trust was shattered. A mood of near despair gripped the territory." The stock market fell 30 percent. To refuse to meet Qian, Major reasoned, would be "no more than a piece of public-relations posturing that would remove any leverage we had to help Hong Kong."

Major wrote that the meeting with Qian prompted him to reflect on how governments must do good by stealth. He reasoned that if he had stated publicly that he wanted to ensure that Chinese troops did not behave in Hong Kong the way they had in Beijing, the truth would simply have created more uncertainty. Would going public about the desire to restore world confidence in Hong Kong have made a bad outcome more likely? This was Major's thinking. In any event, he failed in his attempt to get Beijing to promise that China would not station troops in Hong Kong.

In 1991, Major reluctantly agreed to go to Beijing at the insistence of Percy Cradock, the former ambassador to China and the leader of the negotiating team that produced the 1984 Sino-British Joint Declaration. Cradock, who was so close to Thatcher that he was called "Maggie's Mandarin," was the architect of significant compromises in the negotiations with China, including a British surrender on the validity of the original 1842 and 1860 ceding of Hong Kong in perpetuity. He also persuaded Thatcher not to insist that Britain retain administration over Hong Kong after 1997, when sovereignty would pass to the Chinese. Cradock had secretly visited Beijing in 1989 and 1990, in the wake of the Tiananmen killings, in an effort to foster good relations between the two countries in the transition period before 1997.

An important goal of Major's 1991 trip to Beijing was to convince the Chinese that the British and Hong Kong governments were demonstrating their faith in the post-1997 future of Hong Kong by investing in a new, larger airport that Hong Kong had long needed to cement its position as one of Asia's most important trade and transport nodes. There had been talk for years of replacing the colony's overcrowded Kai Tak Airport. With confidence in Hong Kong plummeting after Tiananmen, Governor David Wilson had announced the so-called Rose Garden airport project in his autumn 1989 policy address. With associated road and rail infrastructure, this centerpiece of Sino-British cooperation was to cost twenty billion dollars. The Chinese insisted that Prime Minister Major personally visit to sign the airport agreement.

Rather than being welcomed by the Chinese as a friend of China, one who was willing to meet the architects of the Tiananmen killings with a view to cooperating on the 1997 handover, Major was met with surly, resentful officials who suspected that the airport project was a British ruse to funnel money from Hong Kong's reserves into the pockets of favored British companies. Cooperation was not on the menu—quite the contrary. Major found himself further humiliated by the Chinese insistence that, although the handover was still six years away, China should have veto power over the airport and other major projects. China effectively wanted to start running Hong Kong immediately. Major was circumspect in his memoirs: About the airport project, he simply wrote that "at the time of my visit they were unwilling to agree to [move ahead]. Only under Chris Patten's gubernatorial guidance was an agreement on the project reached." Privately, to associates, Major was scathing about the Chinese treatment of him on the trip.

The Conservative Party had been in power since Thatcher's victory in 1979. Thatcher's divisive rule had led to her ouster as prime minister in 1990. After ruling Britain for more than a decade, the Conservative Party was widely expected to lose the 1992 election that followed Thatcher's downfall. Instead, John Major's 1992 electoral win was one of the biggest upsets of twentieth-century British politics. Surprisingly, however, the campaign's architect, Conservative Party chairman Christopher Patten, lost his parliamentary seat. Major had planned to make Patten chancellor of the exchequer, one of the top jobs in government and a possible stepping-stone to the position of prime minister. Patten's defeat tempered the sweetness of Major's victory. "Chris Patten's defeat blew a hole in my plans," Major remembered.

Major had a plum consolation prize for Patten: he appointed him as the final governor of Hong Kong. In December 1991, Major had announced that the current governor, David Wilson, would be leaving office within the next twelve months; no successor was announced. Even pro-British Chinese political figures in Hong Kong such as Lydia Dunn and S.Y. Cheung counseled against removing Wilson.[2] They failed to grasp that they would have to take sides. Major was unhappy with his treatment in Beijing the prior September. Wilson, a career bureaucrat, was part of the go-along-to-get-along group of British China specialists who prioritized superficially smooth relations with Beijing. These officials had long used Beijing's aversion to increasing democracy and accountability as an excuse to preserve Hong Kong's colonial system against calls for more democracy. Those calls took on new urgency now that the return of China's sovereignty was imminent.[3] When Major had the chance to appoint the outspoken Patten as governor in an attempt to instill renewed confidence in the people of Hong Kong, Britain's loss became Hong Kong's gain. Patten had a mandate to push for more democracy—exactly the opposite of what Beijing wanted.

Major wrote that his dealings with Beijing were "dominated by one issue: Hong Kong." He appointed Patten as governor, "knowing him well enough to realize he would want to entrench the maximum amount of democracy in the territory before it returned to Chinese sovereignty." Major complained about "the old China hands" who opposed the policy, arguing that such opposition would "poison all our dealings with China, damage Britain's greater commercial and political interests, and disorder the system which had brought about the country's fantastic economic success. They were not alone in their criticism, as British businessmen with contracts at stake (and some Conservative Party stalwarts) queued up to warn me I should not alienate China."

The long colonial twilight that Hong Kong experienced from 1945 to 1997, at a time when other colonies were gaining independence, allowed it room to develop a unique culture, one in which freedom and a free way of life flourished even as political democracy remained extremely limited. For too long, the pace of political developments was controlled by the China experts such as Cradock and Wilson. They were so intent on maintaining relations with China that they failed to grasp how society had changed. Indeed, it was Cradock who had recommended that the anticommunist Thatcher, of all people, become the first Western leader to lay a wreath commemorating China's revolutionary martyrs.

Major and Patten and elected politicians realized that a more prosperous and better-educated Hong Kong people deserved a government that more fully represented them. In his memoirs, Major wrote:

> It was right that as Hong Kong changed, its constitution should change too. Throughout the 1960s and 1970s the colony had a low-cost manufacturing base, with no demand for political reform. By the 1990s it was a prosperous, educated financial center of global importance, and expectations were far greater. The citizens of Hong Kong were now eager for political reform and it would have been wrong to deny it.[4]

No matter the expectations of a prosperous, well-educated city, Major and Patten faced significant opposition from powerful interests. Colonial authorities and the local business community, often with support from Chinese authorities, had repeatedly frustrated moves toward democracy. They had scuttled a plan by Governor Mark Young to introduce more democratic representation in the wake of World War II and had tamped down talk of change after riots in 1966 and 1967. The government conducted surveillance and harassment of pro-democracy activists who began meeting in the 1970s and, supported by the business community and pro-Beijing forces, continued to fight against political liberalization in the years following the 1984 Sino-British Declaration.

Hong Kong's capitalists and Beijing's Communists, with help from the Sinologists in the Foreign Office, formed a powerful anti-democracy alliance. The business community had become adept at hiding its aversion to democracy behind the Foreign Office and the so-called old China hands led by Cradock and Wilson. Patten's biographer, Jonathan Dimbleby, aptly summed up the situation in the early 1990s:

It was clear to any close observer that long before the arrival of Chris Patten, the business community in Hong Kong found themselves in collusion with Beijing against democracy, a situation tacitly but powerfully endorsed by their international counterparts. This was not so much because they feared a Chinese démarche against the subversive threat allegedly posed by the democratic aspirations of their fellow citizens, but because they detected from the same source an equally insidious political threat to their established position as Hong Kong's ruling elite. Their overriding concern was that a new governor, driven by other imperatives, would upset the delicate balance of power in Hong Kong which, for several decades, had given them an effective veto on political and social progress and had preserved their financial and trading citadels intact.[5]

Attempts to get public soundings were fixed to justify a predetermined outcome. A notorious case occurred in the 1987 Green Paper, a form of public consultation, that asked the public about the prospect of democratic elections. A total of 368,431 individuals gave an opinion. Of these, 265,078 were in favor of direct elections. In a blatant attempt at rigging the result, the Hong Kong government, on the orders of the Foreign Office, deliberately misrepresented the results. Each of the tens of thousands of preprinted cards, handed out by pro-Beijing United Front forces opposed to direct elections, were counted as a vote against direct elections. But the signatures on the pro-democracy petitions would not be counted as individual submissions. So, a petition with dozens or hundreds of signatures would be counted as a single submission in favor. The government was thus able to claim that "more were against than in favor of the introduction of direct elections in 1988."[6]

By the time of the handover, Major later wrote with some satisfaction, "Our former colony was in sparkling shape." He noted that from 1992, the year of Patten's arrival, to the time of the handover, the economy had not suffered from the tough negotiations to make Hong Kong more democratic or from China's characterization of Patten as a "strutting prostitute," a "tango dancer," and a "serpent."

Pointing to solid growth in investment, gross domestic product, and exports, Major looked back on a prosperous conclusion to British colonial rule.

The Chinese saw it differently. The seeds of the tangled relations between China and Britain had been planted 150 years earlier; they flowered in the mistrustful post-Tiananmen years. Into those uncertain, pre-handover years the United States inserted itself with the passage of the 1992 United States–Hong Kong Policy Act. The law allowed the United States to treat Hong Kong as a separate customs territory after the 1997 handover, meaning that exports of sensitive technology to Hong Kong would not be subject to the same controls as those to the mainland—provided Hong Kong passed regular reviews confirming that it remained autonomous, as the mainland had promised. China complained that the act constituted interference in its sovereign affairs.

The legacy of Tiananmen continues to haunt China. It is a continuing reminder of the brutality with which the Communist authorities in Beijing will unapologetically act in order to maintain their hold on power. The uncompromising attitude Beijing displayed in the wake of the killings, even to longtime international supporters such as Nixon, did not augur well for Hong Kong.

TEN

THE LAST GOVERNOR

"A THOUSAND-YEAR SINNER"

Chris Patten marked himself out as different from the moment he arrived, declining to wear the ceremonial feathered headdress that British governors traditionally sported, describing the hat as looking as if it had "a chicken on top."[1] It wasn't just the missing plumed hat that showed he was cut from different cloth than his predecessors. The day after he arrived, he went on a walk of a sort that none of them had undertaken in a century and a half, strolling the streets of Mong Kok, a dense working-class area of the colony, holding babies, and accepting petitions from protesters.

Patten came armed with a mandate to make up for 150 years of British neglect toward political reform—to the extent that the remaining five years of British rule made this feasible. One of the most powerful strands of the Communist Chinese narrative about Hong Kong is that the British did not care about democracy during the first 151 years of colonialism. As with every myth, there is some truth to the charge. Percy Cradock, David Wilson, and many of their peers and predecessors were not much interested in democratic reform.

But some in the colonial government had long wanted more

democracy for Hong Kong. The shock of British surrender to the Japanese in 1941 and the searing experience of three years and eight months of Japanese occupation had brought the Chinese and British together on a more equal footing. Many officials spent the war years, both in London and at the Stanley Internment Camp in Hong Kong, thinking about how to develop a new, more democratic and inclusive Hong Kong after the war. Resistance efforts by the British Army Aid Group, made up of Chinese and British, which helped prisoners escape Hong Kong to the safety of free China, forged powerful ties. In 1946, Governor Mark Young's constitutional reform proposals to open up the political system would have been a step in the direction of more democracy. It was an opportunity lost. Politicians and crusaders both in Hong Kong and in Britain regularly pushed for reforms to improve education, working conditions, and health—and the mainland Chinese, as early as the 1950s but especially after the 1984 Sino-British Declaration, consistently pushed back. They were reluctant to recognize that Hong Kong had changed and that the aspirations of the colony's people extended beyond having a job, food, and a place to live. And they wanted political control of the sort that they had on the mainland.

It would have been hard to find anyone in the British government who was better suited to lead Hong Kong in these final years, to help nurture and channel the aspirations of an increasingly prosperous and well-educated community, than Patten. Unlike any of his twenty-six predecessors, Patten was a retail politician, one who had his start in politics working for the successful 1965 New York City mayoral campaign of the young, charismatic Republican—he would switch to the Democratic Party in 1971—reformer John Lindsay. ("He is fresh and everyone else is tired," ran the campaign's unofficial motto.) "What turned me on to politics was getting a traveling scholarship to the USA," Patten wrote later. "In New York, I got involved in the mayoral campaign of John Lindsay . . . and I got the bug."[2]

Patten consciously set out to build popular support among the people of Hong Kong. Biographer Jonathan Dimbleby notes, "The prospect that Patten might use public opinion as a diplomatic weapon, an informal court of appeal, was almost as distasteful to Hong Kong's elite as it was alien to the gerontocracy in Beijing."[3] His walks through the colony, which often included stopping at a favorite store selling a local specialty, egg tarts, won him widespread support from ordinary people. He was the only governor to have a widely recognized nickname, "Fat Pang," or "Fatty Patten," a name that reflected Cantonese earthiness and one that he wore with his characteristic good humor. Patten appointed a pair of younger women, Anna Wu and Christine Loh, who had been part of the pro-democracy camp, to the Legislative Council. He named Anson Chan as his number two, the first Chinese and the first woman to hold the position. He proposed an electoral reform bill that diluted the power of the handful of people who voted for the special-interest seats reserved for bankers, lawyers, accountants, and chambers of commerce. This reform opened the way for the pro-democracy camp, which commanded the loyalty of most Hong Kong voters, to gain more representation.

The Chinese were suspicious of Patten from the start. Most British diplomats in the post-1949 Communist Chinese era, often Sinologists in awe of China's long history, were solicitous of Chinese feelings. Beijing had been used to wielding informal veto power over key Hong Kong decisions, especially since the 1984 Sino-British Joint Declaration. That was the principle that the Chinese insisted on when Prime Minister John Major visited Beijing. Patten, however, simply informed the Chinese of his expected political proposals; he did not seek Chinese approval. Vice Premier Zhu Rongji—later to become the most effective reformer after Deng Xiaoping in Communist China's history—said in London that if Patten proceeded with reform, China could simply do away with the 1984 Sino-British Declaration. China, Zhu threatened, was ready to rip up an international treaty.

Patten ignored the warnings, announcing his electoral reforms in his October 7, 1992, annual policy address. If he won the Legislative Council's approval, the changes would take place in the 1994–95 elections and would effectively bring something approaching universal suffrage to Hong Kong. The Chinese reacted with fury. Patten's Chinese interlocutor, Lu Ping, called him a "thousand-year sinner." Interminable talks between the two sides followed—seventeen rounds in the end. They wound up with no agreement. The Chinese abandoned their idea of a "through train," the notion that legislative and administrative bodies would continue unchanged after the handover. Under the "through train," the governor would have been replaced, of course, as would the flag, but otherwise, the transfer of sovereignty would have been little more than an administrative formality. The Basic Law had been explicitly written to guarantee that Hong Kong's freedoms and way of life would remain largely unchanged for fifty years. Indeed, the Basic Law promised that there should be more freedom, given its promise of universal suffrage.

Such were China's soothing promises, designed to calm a nervous population. Patten called the Chinese's bluff. China's angry response was to do away with the through train and set up a self-styled "separate kitchen," with its own Provisional Legislative Council of handpicked members. Sino-British relations went from wary to downright hostile, showing Hong Kongers the sort of bare-knuckle politics they could expect from China after 1997.

Patten brought more than democratic reforms to the colony. He also focused attention on environmental protection and social welfare. Both concerns reflected his experience as a democratically elected politician. As secretary of the environment under Thatcher, he had spearheaded important environmental legislation in 1991, the year before he came to Hong Kong. Indeed, in his landmark 1992 Hong Kong policy address, where he laid out his proposals for democratic reform, he stated that he had two priorities while in office: more democracy and more environmental protection. He embarked on a multibillion-dollar spending program to clean up Hong Kong's spectacular harbor. (At the time, about 90 percent of the colony's sewage was dumped, untreated or with minimal treatment, into the harbor and other coastal waters.) He also embarked on a large increase in social spending.

Patten's predecessor, David Wilson, was part of the coterie of officials whose encyclopedic knowledge of Chinese politics and history may have blinded them to the changes that were now taking place in Hong Kong and China and that allowed them to shy away from the tough decisions that needed to be made. Certainly, Wilson's expertise was undoubted. He had studied Mandarin at the University of Hong Kong from 1960 to 1962, taken a hiatus from government to edit the *China Quarterly* at the University of London's School for Oriental and African Studies, and had been a political adviser to long-serving reformist Governor Murray MacLehose from 1977 to 1981. Wilson, fluent in Mandarin and proficient in Cantonese, headed the British working group that negotiated the 1984 Sino-British Joint Declaration on Hong Kong and was the first senior British representative to the Sino-British Joint Liaison Group that was set up under the terms of the Joint Declaration. When his predecessor Edward Youde died suddenly in December 1986, while on a trip to Beijing, Wilson took over as governor.

Although democracy advocates criticized Wilson, he did preside, in September 1991, over the first direct elections to the Legislative Council after 150 years of British colonialism. The pro-democracy camp won a landslide victory, securing 60 percent of the vote and sixteen of the eighteen geographic seats. The two most prominent pro-democracy candidates, lawyer Martin Lee and unionist Szeto Wah—who had been called "subversives" by Beijing and expelled from the Basic Law drafting committee—won the highest vote totals. The conservative and pro-Beijing camps—they were more distinct from each other in 1991 than they are today—won 15 percent of the vote, while independents of various stripes took 21 percent of the total. Three decades later, roughly 60 percent of the population continues to support pro-democracy candidates, despite Beijing's opposition.

These elections were the first time that every adult could vote for representatives in the Legislative Council, or Legco, the Hong Kong equivalent of a city council. But the system was rigged in a way that ensured that power could not shift to the camp that plainly had the allegiance of most Hong Kong voters—the pro-democracy camp. Despite winning sixteen of eighteen directly elected seats, the democrats could not control the Legislative Council. That is because under a deliberate pro-establishment and pro-business bias built into the legislature, seats were reserved for what are called "functional con-stituencies." Banking had its own representative, as did accountants, teachers, lawyers, and doctors. In all, there were twenty-one func-tional constituency seats. Their members were elected in some cases by just a few hundred electors, as opposed to the geographic constitu-encies, whose electors numbered in the many tens of thousands.

Almost 1.4 million people voted in the geographic constituen-cies for the eighteen representatives. Just 22,284 voted to elect the twenty-one functional constituency electors; here, conservatives and pro-Beijing forces, as well as independents, did well. The government appointed another twenty-one members to Legco, including the chief secretary, the financial secretary, and the attorney general. In an article written shortly after the election, scholar Ian Scott contended that the 1991 elections were designed as "a sop to democratic senti-ment, a concession designed to ensure that conservative business and professional elites in collaboration with senior civil servants would remain the key decision-makers."[4]

Even before the election, the government itself tried to discredit the expected pro-democracy results, saying that only about 50 percent of people had registered and, of those, only half might show up. Scott detailed government attempts, some of them subtle, to discourage people from voting. When the votes were tallied, large parts of the colony's establishment, badly out of touch with popular opinion, had a hard time accepting the results. The Hong Kong government, China, and the *South China Morning Post* said that the results were not representative. Lu Ping, head of the Hong Kong and Macau Affairs Office and a key official in the handover, said that "people in Hong Kong will sooner or later be able to see clearly what is real democracy."[5]

Scott was quite clear about what the elections meant:

> The Hong Kong voter delivered the unequivocal message that the territory should have an autonomous, free and democratic fu-ture untroubled by interference from the Chinese government....
> But that is not the way in which the political die have been cast.
> The Chinese government has set itself against future constitu-

tional changes for more directly elected seats. It has declared that it has the right, and will actively exercise that right, to intervene in Hong Kong affairs before and after 1997. The 1991 elections results show that, if the Chinese government chooses to take this course of action, it will do so against the democratically expressed wishes of the Hong Kong people.[6]

China even today continues to insist that the British did not want to see democracy in Hong Kong: "In 150 years, the country that now poses as an exemplar of democracy gave our Hong Kong compatriots not one single day of it," *People's Daily,* the official Communist Party newspaper, said in a 2014 editorial. "Only in the 15 years before the 1997 handover did the British colonial government reveal their 'secret' longing to put Hong Kong on the road to democracy." In fact, China had consistently frustrated attempts at political reform in Hong Kong.

As far back as 1958, with the People's Republic less than a decade old and at a time of few diplomatic exchanges, the Chinese moved to deter any British efforts to extend the same sort of democratic freedoms to Hong Kong that it did to colonies that had been granted independence. That year, Zhou Enlai warned Prime Minister Harold Macmillan through an intermediary that China would not tolerate any attempts to institute greater democracy in Hong Kong or to confer on the colony a semi-independent status of the sort that dominion states such as Australia and Canada enjoyed. Zhou claimed that a "plot, or conspiracy, was being hatched to make Hong Kong a self-Governing Dominion like Singapore." China's leaders explicitly wanted to "preserve the colonial status of Hong Kong" and would regard "any move toward Dominion status as a very unfriendly act."

Zhou, who wanted this "very important point" conveyed directly to Prime Minister Macmillan, added that:

[T]he plot was being hatched not by the people of Hong Kong, who were quite satisfied with present conditions, but by Upper Circles [in the British and Hong Kong government], assisted by Chiang Kai-Shek and the Americans. The latter believed they could take a self-Governing Hong Kong within their own orbit. The enormous American Consulate-General in Hong Kong was merely a base for subversive activities in China, and this would become worse if Hong Kongers were self-governing.[7]

Zhou's warning was transmitted through Kenneth Cantlie, a British engineer with long-standing China connections who acted as a high-level intermediary at a time when the two countries had no formal diplomatic relations. (Cantlie's father had been the medical school professor of Sun Yat-sen, the founder of modern China, in Hong Kong and later saved Sun's life when the young revolutionary was imprisoned in the Chinese legation in London; Sun later became Kenneth Cantlie's godfather.) Liao Chengzhi, a senior Chinese official in charge of Hong Kong affairs, said in 1960 that China "shall not hesitate to take positive action to have Hong Kong, Kowloon and New Territories liberated" should the status quo (i.e., colonial administration) be changed. The Chinese threats helped ensure that there would be little democratic development until after Thatcher's 1982 visit to Beijing.[8]

The People's Republic of China joined the United Nations in 1971. Almost as soon as it did so, displacing Taiwan, China moved to have Hong Kong and Macau excluded from a list of colonial territories that should be decolonized. China's ambassador to the United Nations, Huang Hua, declared that Hong Kong and Macau were instead "part of Chinese territory occupied by the British and Portuguese authorities . . . The settlement of the questions of Hong Kong and Macau is entirely within China's sovereign right. . . . The United Nations has no right to discuss these questions."[9]

China's insistence that an exception be carved out for Hong Kong and Macau, saying that they should *not* have a path to self-determination, is ironic for a government that preached the virtues of self-determination for other colonies. With its demand that the two places be removed from the list of Non-self-governing Territories, China won indefinite colonial status for Hong Kong and Macau.

China claims that the United Nations recognized China's sovereignty over Hong Kong. This is, at the very least, stretching the truth.

Delegates voted to approve a work report that was overwhelmingly in favor of decolonization throughout the world, with a single paragraph supporting continued colonization for Hong Kong and Macau. As noted in research by democracy advocate Joshua Wong and coauthor Jeffrey Ngo, this committee report "had five volumes totaling 1,198 pages, of which only paragraph 183 on page 64 of volume I mentioned the question of Hong Kong and Macau."[10] Wong and Ngo continue: "It is manifest, based on verbatim records of the plenary meetings in which the resolution was discussed, that most—if not all—representatives of member states who voted for the resolution did so because they wished to see without delay the liberation of colonized peoples; it was not a vote on Huang's demand."[11]

✿

Patten himself continued to remain immensely popular in the colony. He returned to Hong Kong on several occasions after 1997, greeted by well-wishers as he strolled the streets and visited the East-meets-West Cantonese specialty egg tart shop in Central that he had made famous. I met him only after he left office—the first time, when I moderated a discussion with him sponsored by the American Chamber of Commerce audience in a hotel ballroom jammed with hundreds of people. Among the audience dominated by conservative businesspeople were those who might have been dubious of Patten's reforms at the time of his governorship, but who, with the coming of Chinese rule, had developed a new appreciation for democracy.

More memorable was our lengthy interview in 2005, after he gave a talk at the University of Hong Kong. Patten's speech took place at the historic Loke Yew Hall in the original building of the century-old campus. Afterward, I had arranged for a car to take us the short distance up a hill to May Hall, where the Journalism and Media Studies Center is located, and where I interviewed Patten. The drive was just a few hundred yards long, up a steep and narrow campus road, but well-wishers waved. When we got out, a family that had been picnicking held up their young daughter so that she could have a better look at the former governor. Part of this was, of course, the natural attraction to power, as well as historical curiosity—the little girl would one day be able to tell her grandchildren that she saw the last governor of Hong Kong—but there was a warmth and friendliness that was genuine and unlike any I have seen shown toward Hong Kong's subsequent leaders.

After Tung Chee-hwa, the first post-handover chief executive, was forced to step down in 2005, for years afterward, I would see him walking along Bowen Road, a popular pedestrian path near where we both lived. He was always accompanied by two bodyguards. I would often say hello, and he was always friendly in return—we had developed a passing acquaintance over the years—but I never saw anyone else say hello to him. Donald Tsang does not appear very much in public. He spent most of his first years after leaving office fighting corruption charges and was sent to jail, though the conviction was overturned on appeal. I sometimes saw the third post-handover chief executive, C.Y. Leung, at the Hong Kong Club, fawned on by staff and often ignored by members. Signposts throughout Hong Kong's hundreds of miles of hiking trails are inscribed with anti-Leung graffiti, notably "Down with 689," a reference to the slim majority of votes he received from the 1,200-member election committee in 2012, a number that has become Leung's nickname among Hong Kongers.

Hong Kong's fourth chief executive, Carrie Lam, is afraid to be seen in public. She self-pityingly complained, in a leaked 2019 tape, that she was so fearful of the public that she couldn't even go out to the hairdresser. In contrast to Patten, a retail politician who strolled streets eating egg tarts and shaking hands with excited Hong Kongers, we now have, a quarter century later, a chief executive so reviled that she is afraid to go to the hair salon. This is what Communist Chinese rule, what Lu Ping would call "real democracy," has brought.

PART III

SPRINTING ECONOMY, FALTERING FREEDOMS

ELEVEN

CHINA OPENS FOR BUSINESS

After the 1989 Tiananmen Square Massacre, China's economy froze—and Hong Kong felt the chill. Deng Xiaoping had initiated economic reforms in the late 1970s with the establishment of special economic zones, low-tax, low-regulation enclaves intended to attract foreign investors. But a decade later, China's move toward a more market-oriented economy remained tentative. Influential Communist Party elders were hostile to the idea of opening up the economy to private investment, whether from Chinese entrepreneurs or foreign ones. The aging revolutionaries had ousted Hu Yaobang and Zhao Ziyang because of their modest reforms. After the Tiananmen killings, there was worry in Hong Kong and abroad that China would revert to more orthodox Communist economic policies.

Instead, the years after the Tiananmen killings proved a turning point, setting the stage for a period of stronger and more sustained growth. After China endured three years of a weak and uncertain economy, Deng pushed his reform agenda forward with a dramatic Southern Tour during the Chinese New Year holiday in early 1992. The tour lasted more than a month, from January 18 to February 21;

it was a formidable journey for an eighty-seven-year-old. Although Deng's highest formal position in 1992 was honorary president of the Chinese Bridge Association, he was the final decision maker in China. He visited the Shenzhen Special Economic Zone, just across the border from Hong Kong, and other cities in the Pearl River Delta before going to Shanghai. It was Deng's last significant political act before his death five years later, and it succeeded in cementing the economic reform agenda. Throughout the tour, Deng repeatedly expressed his conviction that foreign investment and foreign technology were needed to modernize China. He told officials in Shenzhen that they "should be bolder in carrying out the Reforms and Opening-up, dare to make experiments and should not act as women with bound feet." In a veiled swipe at the leadership duo of General Secretary Jiang Zemin and Premier Li Peng, who had been installed during the 1989 crackdown, Deng urged that "those who do not promote reform should be brought down from their leadership positions" and argued that "development is of overriding importance."

Despite Deng's position as the country's paramount leader, Beijing media initially refused to report on the tour. The first reporting came from Hong Kong media, letting both an international audience and, more important, a Chinese audience know about Deng's message. This was yet another demonstration of Hong Kong's role as a city that was both part of China and yet not, a place that facilitated the free exchange of information and ideas as well as money into and out of the mainland. The first mainland Chinese report came from a Shenzhen paper at the end of March, more than a month after the trip ended.

China prospered and Hong Kong thrived after the Southern Tour. Hong Kong, with a small population and high land prices, had been seeing its competitiveness in manufacturing erode. By promoting economic growth in China, Deng's trip accelerated the relocation of Hong Kong's manufacturing companies to the neighboring Pearl River Delta. By the late 1990s, it was estimated that Hong Kong–owned factories employed some twelve million people in the delta, almost twice Hong Kong's population. Hong Kong was transformed from a manufacturing enclave largely separate from the

People's Republic to one that was increasingly economically integrated with mainland China—an integration that helped its economy but later provided fuel for protesters worried that the city was losing its separate identity.

Deng's Southern Tour, and the desire for everyone to maintain a positive attitude in the run-up to the 1997 handover, set the stage for Hong Kong's golden years. Although factories left, finance flourished, as financial services businesses from around the world came to Hong Kong to serve the China market. U.S. investment banks such as Goldman Sachs and Morgan Stanley, and asset managers like Fidelity and Charles Schwab, law firms, accountants, and other financial services firms crowded into Hong Kong in the mid-1990s and, today, have hundreds of billions of dollars in assets under management there.

※

I moved to Hong Kong four months after Deng's Southern Tour. The colony was still buzzing about the visit. Deng's intervention jolted business executives out of their post-Tiananmen lethargy, despite continuing nervousness over conservative opposition to capitalist reforms within China. Like everyone else, if more quietly, business leaders were uncertain about what 1997 would mean for this capitalist haven. Many companies had made contingency plans. Jardine Matheson, whose founder had instigated the Opium War that delivered Hong Kong to Britain, had relocated its legal domicile to Bermuda shortly after the Sino-British Joint Declaration was signed in 1984.

Tellingly, the maps I bought when I first moved to Hong Kong were blank north of the border. Hong Kong colonial authorities refused to acknowledge the presence of an increasingly vibrant Shenzhen. This blankness reflected an unwillingness on the part of many people to deal with the reality of China. Writing three decades later, now that Hong Kong is part of China, it's hard to capture the sense of how exotic mainland China seemed even to people living in Hong Kong. In mid-1992, just after I moved to the colony, veteran China correspondent Lincoln Kaye, my colleague at the *Far Eastern Economic Review*, burst excitedly into a meeting: "You won't believe what I heard. There was a group of people on the street speaking Mandarin!"

So rare were mainland Chinese visitors in Hong Kong in the 1990s that even an experienced journalist like Kaye, who had lived in Taiwan and had a Chinese wife, could barely contain his amazement. The "Bamboo Curtain," a Cold War label for the demarcation between Communist and capitalist states in Asia, still separated Hong Kong from mainland China. (Fast-forward to 2018, when fifty-one million mainland Chinese visitors came to Hong Kong, almost seven mainlanders for every local).[1]

I made my first visit to Shenzhen shortly after moving to Hong Kong. I took the most common route, a Kowloon–Canton Railway train to the border. The line had opened in 1910 as part of an imperial effort to stem advances by French and other colonial rivals and preserve Hong Kong's position as southern China's most important international port. Hong Kong, it was always recognized, existed only as an entrepôt for China. If Chinese goods were transported by rail to a rival southern port, Hong Kong would be finished. The rail project was backed by Jardine Matheson and the Hongkong and Shanghai Bank, and construction of the Hong Kong side was financed by the colonial government, which considered the project an urgent priority.

Passenger travel had stopped at the border in October 1949, when the People's Republic of China was established. Even in the early 1990s, there were only a few through trains a day to Guangzhou, the former Canton. Most trains stopped at the border station, Lo Wu. We cleared Hong Kong immigration's formalities and walked across a no-man's-land, a bridge that spanned the Shenzhen River. Passing into China, we came upon a vast construction site. The place had a boomtown feel. A new Shangri-La was being built, part of billionaire Robert Kuok's expanding chain of hotels. Construction sites, new retail spaces featuring Hong Kong stores such as Jimmy Lai's Giordano clothing and foreign brands like Nike and Reebok, stood out from more traditional features of Communist China—Mao jackets and cheap Western suits, trishaws powered by two-stroke engines, a few simple restaurants, and only the most basic shops. A chocolate bar was a luxury, a can of Coca-Cola almost unheard of in this China. All that would change as consumerism came to China, starting in Shenzhen and a few other cities.

I traveled to Shenzhen dozens of times in the ensuing years. Every time, I would visit a new or expanding factory. Talk would always be of growth. Sometimes I was driven to a shoe factory or took a boat trip up the Pearl River Delta to a new industrial park; or visited a factory for a telecom company, like Nortel, or a manufacturing plant for IBM. The construction never stopped. But slowly the physical landscape changed, as did the overall atmosphere. There was a sense of permanency. The freeway network was completed. The quality of the offices and apartment buildings differed little from that in Hong Kong, but the structures sold for lower prices. By 2018, a year when I went to Shenzhen eight times, as I looked south to Hong Kong from the top of the world's fourth-tallest building, the 115-story Ping An Finance Center, it was the former British colony that had a sleepy, bucolic look (though, in fairness, much of this was due to greater environmental protection on the Hong Kong side). In the 1980s, visitors to the border observation post in Hong Kong saw mostly rice paddies when they looked north. By 2018, Shenzhen was a thicket of high-rise buildings.

China came to Hong Kong, but the border crossing (with all the immigration formalities) between the former colony and the rest of the People's Republic remained. During the 1990s and 2000s, it became the world's busiest. By 2018, some 250,000 passengers a day made use of the main Lo Wu border crossing. On holidays, as many as 390,000 passed through the checkpoint. Where there had been only a few trains a day to Guangzhou, there was now a high-speed line. In the early 1990s, it took the better part of a day to get to Guangzhou. By 2018, when the high-speed train line opened, the travel time had been cut to forty-eight minutes. Travel time to Beijing, which had been more than twenty-four hours by train, was reduced to eight hours and forty-five minutes.

The Hong Kong and Chinese governments have built bridges and border crossings, often for good economic reasons. In purely economic terms, it is hard to argue against greater integration with the Pearl River Delta, the vast urban sprawl of some seventy million people that stretches from Hong Kong eighty miles alongside the delta's eastern edge to Guangzhou, at the mouth of the river, and then south to Macau, a gambling city with six times the annual take of Las Vegas, on the delta's western side. This is the area, often called the workshop of the world, where China's export manufacturing clustered after economic reforms began in the late 1970s. Initially reliant on low wages, its companies are becoming increasingly sophisticated. Telecom company Huawei is headquartered in the delta, as is the internet giant Tencent. So is the electric car maker BYD (whose largest shareholder for many years was Warren Buffett's Berkshire Hathaway) and BGI, formerly known as the Beijing Genomics Institute, a pioneer in genomic research.

Integrating Hong Kong more fully with the Pearl River Delta was logical and natural. Doing so made good overall economic sense, although the politics were difficult. Hong Kong taxpayers were forced to pay for expensive bridge, road, and rail infrastructure that was used by the Hong Kong elite and their businesses and by mainlanders who wanted to come to Hong Kong.

A bridge linking Hong Kong and Macau and the neighboring city of Zhuhai was an example of a plan that was as much about political opportunism as common sense. The bridge was initially proposed by Gordon Wu in the 1980s. Wu, a Princeton engineering graduate and second-generation property developer, told British prime minister Margaret Thatcher in 1982 that China's track record on keeping its promises was "terrible" and that he worried about the effect of Britain's handover of the colony.[2] Yet he invested in China.

Wu attended Princeton in the mid-1950s and had been impressed by the postwar American infrastructure boom, and particularly the New Jersey Turnpike—his embrace of America would later prompt him to name his son Thomas Jefferson Wu (who was also a Princeton graduate, class of 1994). He would spend his career working on Asian infrastructure projects, especially around the Pearl River Delta. In the early 1990s, he completed the first highway linking Hong Kong and Guangzhou. Wu was the first to propose a bridge across the Pearl River Delta. It was inspired, he said, by the Chesapeake Bay crossing, a combination of bridge and tunnel connecting Maryland and Virginia. Wu had recommended that the bridge be sited farther north, originating near Castle Peak, on the

Hong Kong side, which would make the structure shorter and less expensive. Instead, the bridge was built farther south, where the delta is wider. Political considerations seemingly determined the route of the bridge, which connected the country's only two Special Administrative Regions (Hong Kong and Macau) and the Chinese city of Zhuhai, adjacent to Macau. When the bridge officially opened in October 2018, a number of Hong Kong elite were summoned to Macau for a brief, impersonal opening ceremony presided over by Xi Jinping. Instructed to take the ferry both ways, they had no chance to use the bridge, acting merely as props for Xi Jinping's ceremonial activities. The bridge almost immediately sparked complaints, paradoxically both for the number of mainland visitors it brought in (mostly on cheap package tours, thus doing little to benefit to the Hong Kong economy) and for being a little-used white elephant that had dramatically exceeded its construction budget but one whose low traffic meant that subsidies by Hong Kong taxpayers would be higher than estimated.

Although Wu worried about the Chinese takeover, he emerged as an outspoken critic of expanding democracy in Hong Kong, being another of Beijing's wealthy supporters. In a 2003 discussion at the Chinese University of Hong Kong, he claimed that only 10 percent of Hong Kong citizens paid taxes, while the other 90 percent received subsidized public housing, health care, and education. He worried that if universal suffrage were introduced, the subsidized group and the politicians they voted in would "get not only free lunches, but free dinners and breakfasts." He advocated introducing full democracy over the course of ten to twenty years. That was almost twenty years ago.

Some flavor of the long and ongoing antagonism between the pro-democracy camp and the business community found expression two years later, in 2005, in an attack on Wu by legislator Cheung Man-kwong during Legislative Council hearings:

Furthermore, Mr. Gordon Wu recently said that to fight for universal suffrage by means of a rally is mobocracy. Has Mr. Gordon Wu tried to ask why the people have to take to the streets? Because they have not succeeded in securing universal suffrage under our system after 20 years. Therefore, if people do not take to the streets, no one will believe that Mr. Gordon Wu will give up, of his own volition, the interests he enjoys as the politically privileged. Just think about this: In fact, behind this long-standing system for the politically privileged, there is imperceptible collusion between the Government and business which does not have to resort to violence but can rely on the system to safeguard the inordinate amounts of profits. This is power politics that does not require any violence to suppress people's right to universal suffrage. This is silent suppression. This is genuine mobocracy practiced by the privileged.[3]

For its part, Shenzhen and the surrounding area is no longer merely a cluster of factory settlements. The Ping An building exemplifies the change. Ping An is a financial services company started by Peter Ma, a former farmer who became a driver during the Cultural Revolution. After economic reform began, Ma founded what is today the world's largest insurance company after Warren Buffett's Berkshire Hathaway; it has a market valuation of about $200 billion and nearly two hundred thousand employees.[4]

In fact, as wages in the Pearl River Delta have gone up, factories have moved inland or to lower-wage countries such as Vietnam. Shenzhen is trying to reinvent itself as a design city. This has provided opportunities for people like Jason Hilgefort, an architect from Ohio who was born in 1977. Hilgefort's firm beat out world-class architects, including James Corner (whose Field Operations designed New York City's groundbreaking High Line project), in a 2018 competition for a 600-hectare forest and sports park in Shenzhen. The Shenzhen project is nearly twice the size of New York's Central Park. Other Shenzhen projects that Hilgefort and his partner, Merve Bedir, have worked on involve the repurposing of old factories into bohemian work spaces, the remaking of the Shenzhen waterfront, and the creation of a new urban district in the city's Qinghai area. Nearby, the Japanese architect Fumihiko Maki, winner of the 1993 Pritzker

Prize, built his first project in mainland China, a shopping mall / museum, the Sea World Culture and Arts Museum, which soars over the Shenzhen Bay and symbolically welcomes ferry passengers from Hong Kong.

Shenzhen's rise highlights Hong Kong's precarious position. Hong Kong is nothing on its own. It survives only by being different from mainland China. For a long time, Hong Kong had better infrastructure, but that is no longer the case. The work that Maki and Hilgefort are doing means that Hong Kong is no longer the undisputed leader in areas that appeal to professionals, like good design and a more livable urban environment.

For the five decades before the 1997 handover, Hong Kongers could comfortably look down on the mainland and mainlanders. In the 1980s, they derided mainlanders as "ah Chan," or country bumpkins. The "ah Chan" phenomenon is worth exploring in some detail. In a long-running TV show that started in 1979, "ah Chan" was the nickname of a young Canton-born boy whose family had come without him to Hong Kong some years before. This sort of family separation was common in post-1949 Hong Kong. After two decades, the son, Ching Chan (nicknamed "ah Chan"), managed to find his way to Hong Kong. His university-educated brother and factory worker sister had been brought up there and were steeped in the polite, professional, hard-driving ways of Hong Kong. Ah Chan was most decidedly not. Instead, as summarized by one critic, he "dozes off at work, stays in bed until late afternoon . . . throws bottles out of the windows of high-rise buildings, jumps the line at the immigration office . . . and steals from the jewelry shop he is working in."[5]

Many of those whom Hong Kongers derided as country bumpkins have by now grown rich. There are an estimated one million U.S. dollar millionaires in China. Hong Kongers regard the mainlanders with both fear and loathing. Nowadays it is mainlanders who are coming in to take most of the high-paying finance jobs. Many of them buy multimillion-dollar luxury apartments. Formerly derided as ah Chans, mainlanders are now characterized by Hong Kongers as "locusts."

Yet Hong Kong has been strangely passive about Shenzhen's rise. Jason Hilgefort describes talking to one of Hong Kong's most prominent architects and urban planners about his work in Shenzhen. The man noted with some condescension that Shenzhen seemed to be doing a lot in the architecture and urban design area. "Of course I've never been there," he admitted. The admission astonished Hilgefort, who had worked in places as varied as Rotterdam and Istanbul before moving to Shenzhen/Hong Kong in 2015. Shenzhen is one of the world's most exciting cities for architecture and urban design, yet one of Hong Kong's leading practitioners hadn't bothered to visit.

Deng's Southern Tour and the accelerated economic reforms that followed focused principally on Shenzhen and the Pearl River Delta. Hong Kong's proximity was essential to China's economic development. Although there were other special economic zones, only Shenzhen prospered. China's opening gave Hong Kong a new purpose, a new source of energy and dynamism. Business opportunities generated unprecedented wealth and introduced a degree of internationalization that, even as one of the world's largest traders, Hong Kong had never experienced.

Hong Kong's reintegration with China, and especially with the Pearl River Delta, in some ways represents a return to nineteenth-century imperialism. The Greater Bay Area, China's clunky marketing term for the region, draws on the association with the tech-savvy, forward-looking San Francisco Bay Area, but the story it tells is an old one. Hong Kong was originally set up to serve a China that was being pried open by imperialism. Now a different sort of imperial power, based in Beijing, wants Hong Kong to be the outward-facing part of a regional economy for a China that still needs an international city. China wants to blur the distinction between Hong Kong and its neighbors, making it easier for mainlanders to come to Hong Kong and for Hong Kongers to live and work in the Greater Bay Area. China is mandating this new role for Hong Kong even as it is destroying the freedoms that make the city unique.

Hong Kong has witnessed a heightened version of the problems plaguing rich cities everywhere, with the hollowing out of manufacturing, a diminishing middle class, and the rise of localism and populism. The flowering of the Hong Kong identity sprang in part from a feeling of superiority to mainland Chinese—a feeling that has now been challenged. The upending of Hong Kong's long-standing sense of superiority, coupled with the very real transition in political power that emanated from the 1997 handover to China, provoked a crisis in Hong Kong. In a single generation, Hong Kongers went from sneering at their country bumpkin "ah Chan" cousins on the mainland to being overrun by them.

TWELVE

"THE GREAT CHINESE TAKEAWAY"

Hong Kong's 1997 Chinese New Year parade was intended to kick off the handover year on a happy note. A freak accident on the first day of the Lunar New Year set a more ominous tone. An ill-designed float sponsored by the Better Hong Kong Foundation poisoned the driver with carbon monoxide fumes. Slumped at the wheel, he drove into a crowd of parade watchers along the Tsim Sha Tsui waterfront district. A visiting English tourist, forty-five-year-old Brenda Stevens, was killed, and thirty-one people were injured. Adding to the tragic irony, the Better Hong Kong Foundation had been set up two years earlier by billionaire property developers intent on countering negative publicity about Hong Kong's future under Chinese rule, after *Fortune* magazine ran a cover story headlined "The Death of Hong Kong."

After fifteen years in which it seemed every conversation in Hong Kong touched on the 1997 handover, the day came and went with appropriate fanfare. As Governor Chris Patten and his wife, Lavender, left Government House for the last time, their driver circled the driveway three times in the official Rolls-Royce, heralding an auspicious return.

As Patten drove down from Government Hill to the Tamar naval installation, threatening skies began to pour rain. At Tamar, an elaborate lion dance was performed, and a Chinese orchestra played. Tamar was the former British naval yard that had been shuttered in the wake of the 1956 Suez crisis, when Britain pulled back from Asia. It was therefore a fitting place to stage the final retreat from Britain's last significant colony. The event was characteristically British; as rain soaked the parade ground, the ceremony continued as planned—it would have been canceled only if it had been raining when Patten left Government House. The rain increased in intensity as the ceremony went on. Patten told the crowd that it had been "the greatest honor of my life" to be the colony's governor. "Now Hong Kong people are to run Hong Kong," he told the crowd. "That is the promise, and that is the unshakeable destiny."

Prince Charles delivered a speech as the rain lashed down, waving away an aide who offered to hold an umbrella. The prince stood erect and alone in his formal white naval dress, proclaiming that although the British flag would be lowered for the last time after more than a century and a half of British administration, "Britain is not saying good-bye to Hong Kong." Red-uniformed schoolchildren ran along Prince Charles's and Patten's Rolls-Royce as it drove away from Tamar. (These children's generation would produce the protesters of the twenty-first century; Joshua Wong was then less than nine months old.)

At midnight, inside the newly built Hong Kong Convention and Exhibition Center, kilted Scots Guards played "God Save the Queen" as the Union Jack came down before the five-starred People's Republic of China flag was raised. Although they were inside, the flags appeared to be waving, thanks to an elaborate system of fishing line that had been rigged to give the illusion that they were flapping in the wind. Even inside the new convention center—built by Henry Cheng, the billionaire property developer behind the Better Hong Kong Foundation—the elements could not be kept at bay. Despite being indoors, Susan Lim, a Singaporean Chinese colleague who directed the crew handling the fishing line that kept the flags flying smartly for photographs, remembers the leaky roof and puddles of water around which VIPs needed to be directed.

I mention the rain because we all seemed to be soaking wet all the time. The ink on my passport was forever blurred after that rain-lashed Tamar ceremony. It rained a total of fourteen inches in those two days. It turned out to be the wettest June and July on record. Everyone seemed to have their own idea about why the skies opened so dramatically. Commenting on Prince Charles's farewell speech, some said that the heavens were intent on washing away the stains of a century and a half of colonialism. Others, thinking of the four thousand PLA troops who stood ramrod-straight in the back of open trucks driving across the border from Shenzhen to Hong Kong the next morning, maintained that the gods were crying for the loss of one of the world's most phenomenal cities. Whatever the reason, a staggering five feet of rain fell in those two months, one third again as much as the annual average for New York City.[1]

At midnight on July 1, 1997, the now-former governor dispatched a telegram to London: "I have relinquished the administration of this government. God Save The Queen. Patten." Inside the convention center, Chinese president and Communist Party general secretary Jiang Zemin gave what he described as a "solemn" speech, proclaiming that the day was "both a festival for the Chinese nation and a victory for the universal cause of peace and justice." Intoning words that few people believed, Jiang continued: "[T]he Hong Kong compatriots have become true masters of this Chinese land." In leaked diaries published later, Prince Charles described the handover as "the Great Chinese takeaway" and compared the Chinese leadership to "appalling old waxworks."

Prince Charles and Patten boarded Her Majesty's Yacht *Britannia* and headed slowly east across the magnificent harbor to the excited, sad, confused, and uncertain cheers of the crowds along the shore. I was among those at the Royal Hong Kong Yacht Club as the illuminated ship departed Hong Kong. This was one of those rare moments when one is conscious of witnessing the end of one era and the beginning of another. As *Britannia* sailed through the harbor, Jiang was addressing what by then was a mostly Chinese audience:

> Chinese people have never recognized the unequal treaties imposed on them, never forgotten for a single day the humiliating state of Hong Kong under occupation and never stopped their indomitable struggle for state sovereignty and national emancipation. With the passage of time, earthshaking changes have taken place. The rise of the first Five-Star Red Flag at Tiananmen Square showed the world that China had achieved national independence and liberation and embarked on a road to socialism. Thanks to reform and opening-up, a rejuvenated Chinese nation has taken on a completely new look, and its international stature has been greatly enhanced. It is under these conditions and against this historical backdrop that Hong Kong has finally returned to the motherland.

Back in Central District, outside the Mandarin Hotel, I bumped into John Ridding from the *Financial Times*. He had just been at the Legco building. Pro-democracy lawyer and legislator Martin Lee had climbed up a ladder and declared that he would defend democracy. The tension and uncertainty were so high that no one knew if Lee would be arrested that night or in the next few days. From there, I went to the border to watch those four thousand PLA troops stream into the city at dawn, the rain once again pouring down, even harder than at Tamar. Would those troops arrest Martin Lee, often known as the "father of democracy in Hong Kong"? As it turned out, not right away. Lee *would* be arrested, but not for twenty-three years. The long colonial twilight under the British was followed by a long neocolonial squeeze and, starting in 2020, a Communist Chinese crackdown.

When we got back to Central after the hour-long drive from the border, the rain had stopped. It was a quiet holiday morning. The four thousand official guests from forty countries, alongside the many Chinese dignitaries, had gone to hotels and homes to sleep off the festivities. What I remember in the gray, quiet city were the red-and-gold Chinese flags flying everywhere. Though I was bleary-eyed and sleep-deprived, the flags woke me up. More than Prince Charles's speech and the Highlanders beating a retreat, more than the "waxworks" at the convention center, even more than the festively lit *Britannia* leaving the harbor, it was the scores of red-and-yellow Communist Chinese flags throughout Central that hammered home the reality that I was now living under Communist rule. There was the large star, symbolizing the Communist Party, and the four smaller stars symbolizing the four social classes: the working class, the peasants, the urban bourgeoisie, and the national bourgeoisie. The red symbolized the Communist Revolution. Yellow gold is a traditional Chinese imperial color; a new colonialism had arrived.

At the handover ceremony, Hong Kong's new chief executive C.H. Tung spoke of the "wisdom and enlightenment" of Chinese leaders who, he said, "granted us a high degree of autonomy—a situation that is unparalleled anywhere in the world." Tung claimed that "we continue to enjoy all our rights as before . . . [and that] a smooth democratic development is assured." Ironically, given the attacks on Patten's efforts to bring democracy to Hong Kong, Tung claimed that "Democracy is the hallmark of a new era for Hong Kong." He promised that it would be a matter of "Hong Kong people administering Hong Kong." Would it? Or would it be the Communist Chinese ruling Hong Kong? A friend of mine who worked for Fidelity, the mutual fund manager, worried about what would happen if he were in a car accident involving another car driven by a PLA officer. Would he have a chance at justice? He decided not to wait around to find out.

Somehow, the government could not help replicating the old forms of colonialism in a new Communist guise. The British had had the Queen's Birthday Honours List, where the reigning monarch— Queen Elizabeth II for as long as almost anyone could remember— dispensed a dizzying array of arcane awards for service to empire. Now Hong Kong would do the same. On July 2, 1997, twelve recipients were awarded with the Grand Bauhinia Medal. The bauhinia had been chosen as Hong Kong's "national" flower; fittingly, it is a sterile hybrid. I'm surely not the first to note the irony that a sterile hybrid signaling Hong Kong's freedoms and values would not reproduce and take root on the mainland.

❀

On the night of July 1, a $13 million fireworks extravaganza filled the harbor. Organized by the team that had produced the opening and closing ceremonies of the previous year's Atlanta Olympics, the show included pandas and oxen, phoenixes and dragons, Chinese lucky coins, lasers, and what was billed as the world's largest karaoke show, much of it taking place on barges built at Chinese shipyards.

Even before the July 1 fireworks in Hong Kong, the distant rumble of trouble could be heard. On the day of the handover, celebrated as the newly created "Hong Kong Special Administrative Region Establishment Day," the government of Thailand devalued its currency. What might have seemed like a technical matter, of little consequence to anyone outside Thailand, proved the spark that set off one of the world's most far-reaching global economic crises since the 1973 OPEC oil shock. The fall of the Thai baht against the U.S. dollar meant higher prices for imported goods for ordinary Thais. Ominously, it meant higher loan payments for Thai companies that had borrowed in U.S. dollars, as many had done. Thailand had made it easier in the run-up to 1997 for its companies to borrow in foreign currencies. Dollar-denominated borrowing lowered costs, as dollar-based interest rates were lower. That was fine as long as the exchange rate was relatively stable. But when the devaluation hit, companies were hurt. They tended to make most of their sales, and earn most of their revenue, in local currency. Since 1984, it had taken about twenty-five baht to buy one U.S. dollar; after the devaluation, it took about forty baht to buy a dollar. The crunch pushed many companies into deep financial distress.

This would not have mattered if Thailand had been a special case. But throughout the fast-growing, so-called miracle economies of Asia, many companies had been borrowing heavily in foreign currencies. Governments, too, had been seduced by the promise of cheap loans to boost growth. Most countries were importing more than they were exporting, so they needed to keep borrowing more money every year. The assumption was that the loans would generate enough growth—whether for an individual company or for the economy as whole—to produce the corporate profits or the government tax surplus to pay back the loans. But when lenders lost confidence, as they did in Thailand, they stampeded for the exits, rushing to get their money out and refusing to put new money in. This precipitated the Asian financial crisis of 1997–98.

Hong Kong was well managed and had superb public finances. Indeed, on the day of the handover, $22 billion was transferred to the government from a special land fund that had collected proceeds from real estate auctions after the 1984 Sino-British agreement. In all, Hong Kong had $81 billion in foreign currency holdings, one of the world's largest foreign currency stashes and one that was particularly impressive given that it had been accumulated in a city of just 6.5 million people.

Yet not even these foreign currency holdings and a well-deserved reputation for fiscal responsibility could protect Hong Kong. As the crisis rolled through the region, Hong Kong suffered. Interest rates briefly topped 100 percent. The stock market plunged 60 percent. Over the next six years, housing prices fell as much as 70 percent. The economy suffered sixty consecutive months of falling prices. Suicides rose. The famously free-market government stepped in to buy stocks. Disease, too, was a problem. To prevent a global flu outbreak, Hong Kong authorities in late 1997 ordered the slaughter of more than one million chickens.[2]

The chief executive of newly Chinese Hong Kong, Tung Chee-hwa (as the former "C.H." now styled himself), was a businessman from a Shanghainese shipping family. His main qualifications appeared to be some ties with the U.S. political establishment and good relations with the People's Republic of China. China had bailed him out after the shipping company founded by his father came close to going under. Jeffrey Garten, who ran Lehman Brothers' Asia operations in the 1980s, helped restructure Tung's debt-laden shipping empire. Garten, who became undersecretary of commerce in the Clinton presidency, remembers Tung as superbly networked. "What was

People's Liberation Army (PLA) troops welcomed by Hong Kong citizens stand on a military transport truck after entering the former British colony on July 1, 1997.

About 500,000 people joined a July 1, 2003, protest against proposed national security legislation in the territory's largest demonstration since those against the Tiananmen killings in 1989.

Joshua Wong (*center*) and other high school students spearheaded a successful 2012 campaign against government plans to require pro-Communist education.

As the 79-day-long Occupy Central wound down, without concessions from, or even negotiations with, the government, protesters vowed "We'll Be Back."

Passer-by jumps to touch sign protesting against continued curbs on democratic elections displayed on MTR station wall in Admiralty during the 2014 Occupy Central movement.

Barrister and longtime democracy advocate Margaret Ng fund-raising at an anti-government rally on China's October 1, 2017, National Day. Significant amounts of money were raised at protests.

On June 9, 2019, about one million people in Hong Kong joined the first rally against a proposed law to allow extradition to mainland China, kicking off the most sustained uprising against Chinese Communist rule since the establishment of the People's Republic in 1949.

Some of the marchers at a June 16, 2019, demonstration, in which close to two million people took part, gather at a memorial for a protester who fell to his death from the Pacific Place complex in Admiralty.

Black-shirted protesters at the June 16, 2019, anti-extradition rally make way for buses on Harcourt Road in Admiralty. Police violence on June 12 energized protests, even after Hong Kong chief executive Carrie Lam said that she would shelve the extradition bill.

Demonstrators joined a rally organized by the Civil Human Rights Front Place in Central to urge G-20 leaders to put pressure on the Hong Kong and Chinese governments.

Demonstrators escalated their actions with the July 1, 2019, takeover of the Legislative Council chambers. Graffiti defaced "People's Republic of China" on the territory's emblem but left "Hong Kong" untouched.

Scores of so-called Lennon Walls (named after similar ones in Prague at the time of the Communist collapse) appeared throughout the territory and were a way of expressing grassroots political opinions. This one is in an underpass near the Tai Po Market Station in the New Territories.

Blockade of cross-harbor tunnel connecting Kowloon with Hong Kong Island, August 3, 2019.

Confrontations grew increasingly heated, as shown in this August 5, 2019, photo where protesters in Admiralty confront police smoke grenades.

Police fire tear gas at protesters outside government apartments occupied by the disciplined services, such as police, in the northern Kowloon district of Wong Tai Sin on August 5, 2019.

Hundreds of thousands of protesters lined Hong Kong's harbor front, streets, and even mountain trails on the evening of August 23, 2019, in what they called the Baltic Way, inspired by a similar event that occurred thirty years earlier and helped bring an end to Soviet rule in the Baltic republics.

Fires became increasingly common as the summer wore on, such as in this August 31, 2019, photo.

The MTR became a target for protesters, especially after police attacks on protesters inside the Prince Edward station on August 31, 2019. This September 8 photo shows a fire outside the Central MTR station.

Protesters hung a massive banner from the iconic Lion Rock, symbol of Hong Kong's can-do spirit, September 13, 2019.

Secondary school students hold hands as they form a human chain on September 12, 2019, in protest against the extradition bill.

Memorial at Prince Edward Station in mid-September commemorating those who were attacked, beaten, and trampled by police on August 31, 2019 (some protesters were made to lie on the escalator steps while police walked over them).

Defaced People's Republic of China seal at the Hong Kong Macau Affairs Office, the seat of mainland power in Hong Kong, on July 21, 2019.

Activist Joshua Wong in handcuffs, May 2019.

Hong Kong's sleek shopping malls were transformed into protest venues, as seen in this September 2019 photo.

Jimmy Lai, handcuffed for the first time after his arrest on August 10, 2019.

Apple Daily was raided for the first time on August 10, 2019, by 200 armed police.

Even after he left office, Chris Patten, the last colonial governor, remained the most popular politician Hong Kong has ever had.

really amazing was how many people he knew. He knew more people on Wall Street than I did. He had spent a huge amount of his time building relationships with people around the world."

Tung had lived in San Francisco for nine years during the 1960s and had worked for General Electric during his time in the States. In 1996, he founded the Hong Kong Forum, which was affiliated with the Council on Foreign Relations in New York. He was well known to Asian-oriented business leaders and U.S. politicians before he took office as Hong Kong's first post-handover chief executive.

During a difficult restructuring process to save Tung's shipping business, Garten spent almost every day for two years with him. "He never ever talked about China," Garten remembers, though Tung once said that he couldn't write Chinese very well and that he needed to brush up on his reading. "After never talking about China, he made a trip to Beijing." Garten, who had not been to the Chinese capital, was disappointed at not being able to go. "A couple of weeks after he came back, he said, 'The Chinese are coming in.'" Tung asked Garten if he knew Henry Fok, who had evaded Korean War embargoes and smuggled arms into China. China did not forget Fok's help. Fok not only became wealthy but enjoyed the trust of China's leadership.

"The Chinese government never said a word about C.H., but Fok showed up and invested. And C.H. said this was China coming in. I don't know exactly what happened. I don't know if they gave Fok the money, or asked him to do a favor, or guaranteed the money." The Chinese may have been interested in Tung partly because of his strong connection to Taiwan. "He had very strong relations in Taiwan—his family had been there for a long time," said Garten. "His father had been very highly regarded in Taiwan. I recall C.H. saying that the Chinese were interested in him in part because he could be a channel to Taiwan." Garten remembers Tung not only for his cosmopolitanism and his contacts but for his energy, his attention to detail, and his "scrupulous integrity." After the bailout of his company, which allowed Tung to rebuild his wealth, he would be forever indebted to China.

Tung was not a politician, and he displayed an elitist aloofness and rigidity that were completely at odds with Hong Kong's developing political culture, particularly after Chris Patten's retail politicking. When Garten later visited Tung, after he had taken over as Hong Kong's chief executive, Tung professed "no interest in politics." As Garten noted:

> He saw himself as someone who had something to run, something to manage. The management of Hong Kong was an overwhelming task in itself, and the overlay of the politics was [as Tung saw it,] a terrible distraction. I remember thinking that people who are in business even at the highest levels often don't adapt to going into government because they underestimate the overwhelming nature of the politics itself.

Tung was forced to resign midway through his second term after a bungled attempt to introduce national security legislation sparked large-scale protests.

❦

It was with a mixture of pride and fear, anticipation and dread, and in some cases even indifference that the handover took place. Today, with two decades of hindsight, and at a time when the government is distrusted and Beijing widely reviled, it might be easy to imagine that Hong Kong was united in its antipathy to the 1997 handover. But many people genuinely welcomed the end of British rule. If nothing else, after June 30, 1997, we wouldn't have to endlessly wonder about the handover, as had been the case in almost every conversation since I'd moved to Hong Kong five years earlier.

Historian Philip Snow claimed that there were more Chinese flags than British ones on display at the time of the handover. Many, probably most, of those flags were provided by various United Front and government-funded organizations. But to dismiss this sense of patriotism and national pride would be wrong, for there were many who welcomed the promise that they would be masters in their own land.

The business community, however nervously, certainly embraced the idea of making money. The China opening was finally happening, something that business had looked forward to for two centuries. The economy had roared during Patten's time in office, the benchmark Hang Seng Index of stocks more than doubling. The political temperature may have been frosty, but Beijing did everything it could to ensure that the economy remained robust and thereby enhance the feel-good factor.

It is worth pointing out that the Chinese economy's once-in-a-century burst of growth coincided exactly with the handover. Deng's economic reforms—notably the establishment of the special economic zones and the "reform and opening" process—had been announced at the end of 1978; but in macroeconomic terms, the reforms hadn't amounted to much by the time the 1989 Tiananmen killings halted further reform. In some sense, 1978 was a sort of practice start, and Deng's 1992 Southern Tour could be regarded as the real beginning of economic liberalization and internationalization. The entry into the World Trade Organization ten years later, in December 2001, provided the biggest boost of all.

Hong Kong both benefited from and contributed to China's opening. In the 1990s, the first Chinese companies started to list on the Hong Kong stock exchange; in doing so, they had to stop being run simply like party units in a planned economy and become profit-oriented companies with Western accounting standards and other international practices. Hong Kong factory owners expanded their operations in Shenzhen and throughout the Pearl River Delta. Gordon Wu's Hopewell built its highway from Hong Kong to Guangzhou. Rail services were accelerated.

Mainland companies started doing business in Hong Kong. They bought shares in Hong Kong companies. China Investment Trust and Investment Co. (CITIC), headed by Larry Yung, whose family were prominent Shanghai textile manufacturers and whose father was China's former vice president, was particularly active. CITIC bought stakes in the colony's leading electricity company, China Light and Power, in Hong Kong's only significant airline, Cathay Pacific, and in a new cross-harbor tunnel built as part of the airport project. Deng Xiaoping had famously promised that the horses would still run, stocks would still sizzle, dancers would still dance. This wasn't going to be just for Hong Kongers. A horse racing aficionado, Larry Yung became the first mainland Chinese steward at the Jockey Club, one of the colony's most prestigious slots.

The mainland cadres were going to make many fortunes. Would there be anything left for Hong Kong businessmen, let alone for the old-line British companies like Swire, which controlled Cathay Pacific? How much would Jardine be punished, as it was during talks for a new port terminal? Who would profit from Hong Kong's success?

The British bet had been that China was changing and that Beijing could be trusted to live up to its promise of granting Hong Kong a "high degree of autonomy." Malcolm Rifkind, who was Britain's foreign secretary in the two years leading up to the handover, remembers the thinking.

> Until Tiananmen Square the hope was, because that was what was happening elsewhere in the Communist world, in Europe, that Chinese communism would change. [We had seen] Deng Xiaoping's own changes of Chinese internal policy. The Chinese characteristics may have been there but essentially it was an adoption of a capitalist model rather than in a Communist mode. We were hopeful that Chinese communism would change. Hong Kong, if it succeeded, was always going to be there as a potential alternative system. I'm not sure that that was unjustified until Xi Jinping took power.

There were flashes when Rifkind realized how long a road China needed to travel even to begin to understand Hong Kong's system. One time, he visited Hong Kong on his way to talks in Beijing with Foreign Minister Qian Qichen. Even more important than political rights, Hong Kong legislators told Rifkind, "is the rule of law, that our judicial system, that our rights entrenched in law will continue. We have that. China doesn't have that. Could you try to make that clear to the foreign minister?" When he got to Beijing, Rifkind stressed the importance of rule of law to Qian, as urbane and cosmopolitan an official as China had:

I said to him, "I've just been in Hong Kong, and what they're really concerned about when they become part of China again will
be that they continue to enjoy the rule of law." I've never forgotten his answer. He said, "Oh, don't worry, Mr. Rifkind, in China
we, too, believe in the rule of law. In China, the people must obey
the law!"

A quarter century later, Rifkind still remembers the exchange.

I looked at him and I said, "Now hold on, minister, when we talk
about the rule of law, it's not just the people who must obey the
law. It's the government that must obey the law. The government
must be under the law." It wasn't that he didn't agree with me;
he couldn't understand what I was talking about. Democracies
have the rule of law. China and other dictatorships have rule *by*
law. They criminalize even peaceful political opposition. The real
point is not that he didn't agree with me. He couldn't understand
the distinction, the assumption that government should submit
themselves to judges that they themselves would have appointed.[3]

As he left office, Chris Patten asked rhetorically, "Can you gov-
ern Hong Kong well against the grain of public sentiment and as-
piration? Can you deny people what they've been promised? Can
you sell them counterfeit goods when they've experienced the real
thing? Can you take away for good what is the best guarantee of
Hong Kong's much promised autonomy, its decency and stability?"[4]
This would be the challenge for China's leaders, a challenge that the
Hong Kong people would answer emphatically in the decades ahead.

Aspirations for expanded popular participation in politics had been
present for decades. The combination of British colonial caution—
tinged for long with racism—coupled with the Chinese fear of any
sort of democratic awakening and the business elite's long-standing
opposition to any meaningful expansion of political rights all contributed to the popular fiction that, as I heard repeatedly from business leaders during the 1990s, "Hong Kong people don't care about
politics."

Hong Kong people had been promised that political development would be a matter for them to decide on their own, and that, under the Basic Law, they could enjoy universal suffrage beginning in 2007. (The Basic Law permitted but did not require universal suffrage beginning that year; the widespread expectation was that this would be the date at which a real competitive political system could develop.) The proposed election changes were hesitant, halting, and didn't address people's desire to freely elect their mayor and the city council. The government appeared far more concerned with enacting national security legislation, which was mandated under Article 23 of the Basic Law, than in implementing the promises of universal suffrage provided for in Article 68.

What developed in the years after 1997 was a culture of protest. In the absence of democratic elections, large-scale rallies became a way for Hong Kongers to express themselves, individually and as a community. Street protests became a way of protecting Hong Kong's so-called core values—which all centered on freedom—and in turn the protests themselves came to be seen by many Hong Kongers as a core value. They were a means of building community as well as of expressing oneself. This was summed up in graffiti I saw at the University of Hong Kong: "I protest, therefore we are," a play on Descartes.[5]

The years became more crowded with annual protests and commemorations. On July 1, 2003, one of Hong Kong's largest protest marches saw some five hundred thousand people march against proposed national security legislation—fearing the very loss of their liberties that would in fact come after national security legislation was adopted in 2020. Since 2003, in addition to the annual June 4 vigils honoring victims of the Tiananmen killings, there have been annual July 1 marches every year until 2020, when they were prohibited, ostensibly because of COVID-19. July 1 is a public holiday, the Hong Kong Special Administrative Region Establishment Day, so the fact that it has been appropriated by pro-democracy forces is another irritant to authorities. As hope for democracy dwindled, the importance of street protests grew. Hong Kongers couldn't elect their mayor or their city council, but they could build and celebrate a community around the theater of street protest.

THIRTEEN

"THE FIRST POSTMODERN CITY TO DIE"

The idea that a city exemplifying capitalism on steroids was going to be easily reunified with the so-called motherland run by a Communist Party was always preposterous. Hong Kongers had been nervous even before Margaret Thatcher's trip to Beijing in 1982. The difficult Sino-British negotiations of the mid-1980s and the Tiananmen killings of 1989 stoked their fears. Hundreds of thousands immigrated to Canada, Australia, New Zealand, Britain, and the United States. The 1997 handover and its aftermath saw political uncertainty as China moved to assert control. The wooing of the business community took place at the same time as the Chinese used harsh tactics against John Major and Chris Patten, demonstrating who was the new boss. Chinese authorities systematically worked to undermine the institutions that had made Hong Kong a free and open society. Despite, or because of, these unrelenting Chinese efforts, Hong Kong's first four chief executives have failed spectacularly, each in his or her own way. The independence of the legal system has been undermined, the media have been bullied and bent to serve Chinese purposes, and Hong Kong as a free society has been all but extinguished.

Even as China was snuffing out many of the facets that made Hong Kong unique, Hong Kongers themselves were creating their city anew, developing a sense of Cantonese–Hong Kong cultural, social, and political identity that reinvigorated the city and was like nothing the Chinese world had ever seen. (The only parallel was emerging in Taiwan, where five decades of authoritarian rule under Chiang Kai-shek's KMT was giving way to democracy at precisely this time.) After the handover, and especially after the 2003 SARS epidemic, Hong Kong enjoyed a new sense of energy and dynamism. This flowering came even as many ordinary people felt that their city was being overrun by mainland tourists and immigrants and strangled by high property prices. Hong Kongers were particularly frustrated by Beijing's continued unwillingness to allow the city to develop the political freedom it had been promised.

In the wave of decolonization that extended from 1946 (when the Philippines gained independence from the United States) to 1984 (when Britain ceded independence to Brunei), the United States, Britain, France, Portugal, and the Netherlands all surrendered their colonies in Asia. Hong Kong and Portuguese-ruled Macau were special cases. China had acted at the United Nations in the early 1970s to preclude those colonies' possible independence; a restoration of Chinese sovereignty would be the only option. Most colonies wanted their foreign masters out; they wanted freedom and independence. Portugal tried to give Macau back to China in the 1970s. Although China did not follow through at the time, the ultimate fate of the gambling enclave was never in doubt. But Hong Kongers were in no hurry for the British to leave. Most of them or their parents or grandparents had fled from the very same Communist Chinese who were now about to take over. Despite the costs of colonialism discussed earlier, Hong Kongers saw Britain as protection from China's predatory power.

As virtually every other significant colony in the world became independent after 1945, Britain faced pressure to show that it could deliver prosperity and order, if not political freedom, in Hong Kong. British authorities knew that they needed to be responsive, given that a tiny colonial elite ruled a city that was more than 90 percent

Chinese. The mainland could easily seize the colony at any time by cutting off food or water supplies, something far more likely to occur if Britain lost the support of Hong Kongers. Hong Kong colonial authorities responded to the refugee crisis in the 1950s by building public housing and starting a campaign of mass inoculations. They responded to leftist riots and widespread bombings in 1967 with more grassroots accountability and more spending on schools and health care. Britain harnessed the energy of Hong Kong's young population, many of them refugees, to turbocharge economic growth and, in the final decade of colonial rule, expand civil liberties and opportunities for political participation—in short, to build a free and prosperous society.

The British left strong institutions to protect individual liberties. The British legal and governance system, coupled with a light-touch government, allowed an extraordinary economy to flourish. And yet Hong Kong people were not running Hong Kong. To have an alien race, an alien culture, as your ruler is something that few people would want to accept, especially for the heirs of one of the world's most extraordinary and long-lived cultures, one with a more or less unbroken tradition of government administration stretching back over two thousand years.

It wasn't just talk when Tung Chee-hwa celebrated the "wisdom and enlightenment" of China's leaders at the handover ceremony. Tung and his generation had seen the country ripped apart by civil war. The hunger for national territorial integrity gnawed at many Chinese of Tung's generation. Uniting Hong Kong, two years later Macau, and someday Taiwan was an important part of China's reclaiming a central role in Asia and the world. (Think of how Ronald Reagan attacked Jimmy Carter for allowing the Panama Canal to revert to Panama, and the passions that debate stirred in many Americans, for a sense of how even small bits of land can take on disproportionate importance.)

Colonialism is corrosive, even the most benign kind. Britain's Hong Kong colonial subjects had always known the sting of racial discrimination and social snobbishness. It was not until 1949 that the first Hong Kong Chinese, war hero Paul Tsui, was recruited into the Colonial Civil Service. British candidates continued to get preference. The Civil Service started aggressively recruiting local candidates only in the 1980s.

Colonial tactics were harsh. Sixty people were killed during 1956 riots between the KMT and CCP, mostly at the hands of police. Hundreds of leftists were jailed without trial during 1967 anticolonial riots.[1] Meanwhile, corruption in the police ranks, centered on British officers, was so bad that it resembled a racketeering organization. Governor Murray MacLehose had to put down a police mutiny in 1977 when disaffected cops attacked the headquarters of the recently formed Independent Commission Against Corruption.

It was only after the decision to hand the colony back to Beijing that Britain eased its harsh restrictions on political activity. The final years of colonialism were made more poignant by the 1989 Tiananmen killings. As the aftershocks of the Tiananmen massacre continued to be felt throughout China, the prospect of China's taking over was met with very mixed feelings. Many Hong Kongers felt a sense of national pride that the stain of colonialism would be erased and excitement over the opportunities that would come with being part of a fast-growing and changing country. The most honest among the Chinese patriots at the same time had to worry that Hong Kongers' individual freedoms and liberty might be eroded or erased.

A full fifteen years passed between Margaret Thatcher's visit to Beijing in 1982 and the lowering of the Union Jack under the gaze of Prince Charles at midnight on July 1, 1997. Over the course of its 156 years as a British possession, but especially in these final years, Hong Kong developed a dynamic private sector, created world-class infrastructure, and increased its wealth. It did this under the often benevolent colonialism of a system that instilled a belief in rule of law, decent governance, and minimal corruption. This period prepared Hong Kong not, as it turned out, for freedom and democracy, let alone for independence, but for a new colonial master.

Mainland Chinese attempts to mold a new post-British identity for the Hong Kong people struck many as propaganda. Hong

Kongers were expected to go from being colonial subjects to "Chinese," a label that would prove problematic, especially given that "Chinese" was increasingly defined as Communist Chinese. Instead of fostering a Chinese identity, the mainland government succeeded largely in nurturing a stronger sense of Cantonese identity.

Reintegration with China gave Hong Kong a new purpose, a new source of energy and dynamism. Hong Kong's pivotal role in the economic reform and opening up of China led to unprecedented wealth. But many were left behind—economically, socially, and politically. At the same time, China's increasing involvement in Hong Kong created anxiety. What China saw as helpful—namely allowing more mainland tourists and property buyers access to Hong Kong—many or most Hong Kongers saw as a hostile takeover of their city.

Property prices went up further and faster than in any major city in the world, a fivefold increase from 2003 until 2018. Hong Kong also saw a decline in its manufacturing sector, though this was well under way before the handover. Even if China had not been opening, and Hong Kong industrialists had not employed some twelve million people across the border, manufacturing jobs would have disappeared as Hong Kong's higher wages made the city's labor-intensive manufacturing base uncompetitive. Taken together, the loss of good-paying working-class jobs, the quintupling of already-high property prices, and a seemingly unending swarm of mainlanders to shop and take jobs and buy property fed resentment. If there had been democracy, Hong Kong's problems might have been argued out at the ballot box and in the legislature. Instead, the drama would unfold in the streets.

To give Chief Executive Tung Chee-hwa credit, he did try to improve the housing situation. He set a target of building eighty-five thousand new apartments a year. "Hong Kong has enough land to meet our housing needs," Tung proclaimed in his handover speech. The mere fact that this sort of planning target would be a feature of his first speech as chief executive, on July 1, 1997, signaled how the Hong Kong government would move toward a more interventionist approach. Tung's target would have roughly quadrupled the number of new apartments available each year. Just over half of Hong Kongers owned their apartments at the time of the handover. About 40 percent lived in public housing. Tung pledged to speed up construction of government flats that would be sold to the so-called sandwich class, middle-class people who made too much money to qualify for public housing but not enough to afford a down payment necessary to buy an apartment.

Taking a leaf from Margaret Thatcher and Singapore's Lee Kuan Yew—and prefiguring what would soon happen in China—Tung also pledged to sell public housing apartments to sitting tenants. "Owning one's home," said Tung at the handover, "is crucial for nurturing a sense of belonging and maintaining social stability." Due to the financial crisis, which started just as Chinese rule began, virtually none of this happened. Home prices did fall, by as much as 70 percent, as Hong Kong endured six difficult years.[2] The problem was that high land prices continued to suit the government, and a handful of big developers, just fine. The government relied on revenue from land leases to fund spending while keeping personal and corporate taxes low.

Tung's successor, Donald Tsang, artificially crimped land supply just as the economy was entering a period of strong growth after the Asian financial crisis. The government had intended to relocate its headquarters to a run-down area of Kowloon near the old Kai Tak Airport as part of a redevelopment plan for Kwun Tong, a former manufacturing district that had faded as companies moved to China. Instead, Tsang took over the old British Tamar naval base next to Central for the new government headquarters. The property had been intended for commercial development, to provide additional space near the main business district. The government's decision to take the largest remaining development site in the core Hong Kong business district squeezed supply, fueling a further rise in property prices. The large complex at the Tamar site became a monument to big government and a reminder of the lengths to which the government would go to ensure that property prices remained high. Ironically, the Tamar site also meant demonstrations would continue to take place in the commercial heart of the city, at a location that offered easy access for protesters and ensured intensive media coverage.

In the period after 1997, Hong Kong was transformed from a British colonial operation with a remarkable degree of autonomy to one that is now controlled directly by Beijing's Communist Party representatives in the city, China having betrayed Deng Xiaoping's promise of "Hong Kong people ruling Hong Kong." The transition started immediately. As early as 1999, *The Economist* bemoaned "Hong Kong's hazy future" shortly after China blocked a planned visit to the city by the pope. The magazine noted that neither the government nor business did enough to keep the Hong Kong spirit alive. The magazine presciently commented that both "seem not to have shaken off the colonial cringe of those who seek to second-guess the wishes of their distant rulers." It went on to express concern about "death by a thousand cuts" and urged those who say China would not kill the goose that lays the golden eggs to remember Chris Patten's warning: "that phrase would never have entered the language were history not littered with dead geese."[3]

Working-class incomes never recovered after the 1997 Asian financial crisis. Hong Kong workers had to compete with low-paid Chinese ones. It was not just factory workers who felt the pressure of competition. Cross-border truck drivers saw wages fall from almost $4,000 a month in 1997 to about half that ten years later as Chinese ports opened up and there was less demand for their labor. Even in areas where there was no direct competition with China, wages stagnated. The starting monthly pay for newspaper reporters was about $1,150 at the time of the handover and has hardly moved for two decades. The stagnation in wages and living standards at a time when apartment prices were in the midst of a fivefold increase led to a rise in local identity politics and to populism in Hong Kong.

My activist friend Yan, whom I first met at the Easter lunch where he talked about the need for more militant action, contends that rosy official employment statistics mask a rise in unemployment as job growth has stagnated: "It's not just that they are getting paid less; they don't have a job," he said. "Hong Kong has changed so fast in the last five years. We erased the border with China, and hospitality [programs] became such a big thing, completely skewing the economy. Yet now, with the collapse of tourism, a hospitality program degree is worth less than the paper it's printed on."

❀

From a Hong Kong perspective, the increase in mainland visitors from a few thousand a year to fifty-one million in 2018 felt like an invasion. A handful of restaurants put up signs saying mainlanders weren't welcome. There were many complaints about the first waves of tourists, remembers my Cantonese teacher Chan, who lives in the Tuen Mun area of the New Territories, a large New Town (satellite towns developed beginning in the late 1950s) not far from the mainland border and a major tourist destination. There were complaints that mainland tourists would talk loudly—and this is saying a lot, given that Cantonese speakers always struck me as pretty much the world's noisiest talkers—and would "sometimes let their kids shit on the street or while holding the child over a rubbish bin," says Chan. "I remember they spit a lot."

There were other differences. Mainlanders like to squat on their haunches while they are waiting, rather than stand. "I just don't understand why they squat on the street, like at the bus stop. If you see someone squatting, they speak Mandarin. If they are standing, they speak Cantonese." Though Chan says that complaints have lessened in recent years, relations are so antagonistic that pro-Beijing commentators continue to push for the city's antidiscrimination ordinance to include anti-mainland discrimination. If, as the official Communist narrative maintains, almost everyone in Hong Kong is Chinese (a story line that seeks to minimize differences), how could it be possible for Chinese to discriminate against Chinese?[4]

There is intense discrimination, but it is cultural and linguistic rather than racial. It has worsened in recent years. In the quarter century since the handover, Hong Kongers have cultivated their sense of identity. Rather than basking in the pride of being Chinese, they have celebrated being Hong Kongers—and part of being a Hong Konger is not being a mainlander. The sense of Chinese identity peaked around the time of the 2008 Beijing Olympics. Nowadays, in surveys, fewer describe themselves as Chinese and more describe themselves as Hong Kongers.

Most people in the city speak Cantonese as their mother tongue, underscoring the sense that Hong Kong is special, a place somehow distinct from the rest of China. Although the written characters in Cantonese and the mainland's national language, Putonghua (also called Mandarin), are similar, the languages are as distinct as Swedish and English. Hong Kongers used to joke that when a Putonghua speaker conversed with a Cantonese one, it was like a duck talking to a chicken. No one is joking anymore.

Language has emerged as an important factor in distinguishing Hong Kong from mainland China, and linguistic differences have come to loom large in the growing tension between the two. I studied Mandarin most of the time I was in Hong Kong, with a few desultory attempts at Cantonese. During my final years in the city I made a more serious attempt to learn Cantonese. Although my Cantonese never became very good, during that time I had two teachers who taught me a lot about the importance of Cantonese in the development of Hong Kong's identity. Chan was one, and Lau Chaakming the other. I met Lau in 2015, a year before he started working on his doctorate in Chinese linguistics at the Chinese University of Hong Kong, when he taught a Cantonese class at the University of Hong Kong. Lau had studied in Japan, where he first realized how poorly regarded Cantonese was internationally. The year before I met him, he launched an audacious project to compile the first-ever Cantonese–Cantonese dictionary. This is for native speakers—like Webster's for an American—in contrast to a bilingual dictionary for learners from another language.

"I am trying to make Cantonese great again," he told me. Great again? Lau reminded me that Cantonese had been the predominant language among the overseas Chinese communities of Southeast Asia and a source of significant cultural influence, through film and music, in East Asia during much of the middle and late twentieth century.

To understand the importance of the dictionary project and the role Cantonese plays in Hong Kong's development requires a detour into a discussion of Chinese languages, which include not only Cantonese and Mandarin but languages in five other distinct linguistic groups. Indeed, these regional variations are so pronounced that mainland Chinese TV news shows feature subtitles.

The attempt by the Chinese government to impose a standard national language is part of a process of political control and centralization, just as it was earlier in countries like France and Italy as they became nations. Cantonese, although it is also spoken in much of neighboring Guangdong Province and nearby Macau, has emerged as a marker of Hong Kong identity. For a more recent European parallel, think of how language was used to nurture local identity in the Catalan- and Basque-speaking regions of Spain.

Chinese is a logographic language, one that relies on symbols rather than a phonetic alphabet. Some of the characters are pictograms or ideograms, visually representing an object, although most are abstract. Often the characters have the same meanings, but different pronunciations, across the Chinese-language family and even in Japan, Korea, and Vietnam. For example, the character for "person" looks like a stick figure. The same character is used in both Mandarin and Cantonese, but it's pronounced *ren* in Mandarin and *yan* in Cantonese. So, someone from Beijing could understand the character if they read it in a Hong Kong newspaper, though the Hong Kong reader and the Beijing reader would, of course, pronounce it differently. This leads to curious scenes where one sees speakers from different Chinese languages writing characters to communicate with one another when speech is mutually incomprehensible.

The similarities end pretty quickly. Not only is pronunciation of the same characters quite different in different forms of Chinese, but different characters are often used to express the same meaning in different Chinese languages. The character for "no" is altogether different in Cantonese and Mandarin. So is the character for "he/she." (In fact, Cantonese is extremely unusual, if not unique, in making no gender distinction in either the written or spoken "she/he.") Mainland China has simplified many characters, increasing the difference between the two languages.

Chinese is a tonal language, and Mandarin has four tones while

Cantonese has six (or, in some regional variations, nine or more). Spoken Cantonese is largely incomprehensible to a Mandarin speaker. Imagine an American listening to a German speaker—there are cognates, and many words sound familiar, but these are two different languages. A Swedish speaker can understand a Norwegian one better than a Beijinger can understand a Hong Konger.

It's often said that a language is a dialect with an army and a navy. The mainland Chinese government insists that Cantonese and other regional languages are dialects, implying that they are variants of the true Chinese language, Putonghua. It encourages citizens in Guangdong Province, which borders Hong Kong, to be "civilized" and speak Mandarin Chinese. Classes in mainland schools are taught in Mandarin, and Hong Kong is moving in that direction.

Although Cantonese has dominated Hong Kong's core urban areas for over a century, it became the common language colony-wide only in the years after the end of World War II. Two other forms of Chinese, Hakka and Waitou, were widely spoken in the New Territories until the 1980s. The first free-to-air local television broadcaster, Television Broadcasts, or TVB (founded in 1967 by the improbably named Chinese movie producer Sir Run Run Shaw), is credited with building a Hong Kong linguistic identity.

For many years, newspapers used only standard written Chinese—Mandarin. So, the written language didn't bear much resemblance to how people spoke. Like many children in America who grew up before the internet, I started reading the newspaper in elementary school. That would have been impossible for my Hong Kong counterparts. It would have been like giving me a Latin Bible to read. "Primary school students would have no chance of understanding newspapers," says Lau.

This started to change in the run-up to the handover in the 1990s. Jimmy Lai's *Apple Daily* started using Cantonese slang in the newspaper. On a small scale, *Apple*'s editors did for its Cantonese readers something similar to what the King James Bible did for everyday Christians in England. Traditional newspapers were accessible only to the educated elite. *Apple* was a newspaper whose lighter stories, at least, were written the way people talked, in earthy Cantonese slang.

To write down what had been solely a spoken language, editors often added a "mouth" symbol on the left side of a character that sounded the same as the spoken word, to alert readers that the character represented a sound rather than its original meaning.

Other newspapers followed suit—but not the pro-Communist papers. Even now, Hong Kong's leftist papers, which adhere to Beijing's policies, don't use Cantonese words or slang in their news stories or opinion columns. They do quote Cantonese—especially written Cantonese from the pro-democracy camp—adding a translation next to Cantonese words.

᙭

Lau's dictionary project aimed to give Cantonese a status that it had not enjoyed before, putting it on a scholarly par with the national language. The crowd-sourced dictionary has fifty thousand entries, compared with seventy thousand for China's national dictionary. As well as standard Cantonese speech, the dictionary collects slang, unlike the mainland's, and Lau thinks that the project can double its entries within the next decade. The project has a thousand contributors, with Lau among a core group of twenty.

Putonghua-language instruction has increased significantly in Hong Kong's schools since the 1997 handover, and some people worry that there is a concerted attempt to wipe out the Cantonese language, along with the distinctive local culture. One of the five segments in the 2015 hit movie *Ten Years* features a Cantonese taxi driver who is unable to learn Mandarin and loses his livelihood, and his daughter's affection, as a result. In reality, the effect of increased mainland pressure has been to strengthen Cantonese. Shortly before the 2014 Umbrella Movement started, I gave a taxi driver directions in Mandarin. "I don't understand," he said to me in English. *Duibuqi* (I'm sorry), I replied in Mandarin. "My Cantonese is no good." Again, he countered my Mandarin with his English: "We don't speak that language here." In fact, that's not true. Most Hong Kongers have learned enough Mandarin in the past quarter century to be able to understand their mainland cousins, but they don't like it. Mainland China feels like another colonizing power.

Many movements seeking greater autonomy have placed language at their core. Think of the Basque, the Quebecois, and the Irish. The periodical *Resonate* is the first attempt at a serious literary magazine written exclusively in Cantonese. "Supporters of Cantonese tend to be supporters of freedom, democracy, and local rights," Lau, now a professor at the Education University of Hong Kong, told me. He insists that the dictionary is not a political project. "We try not to politicize everything. We don't want to exclude users from different political views. We try to stay neutral."

The Chinese government certainly seems to think that Cantonese matters and has taken extraordinary steps to ensure that the language does not continue to develop. Chinese negotiators have worked to marginalize it by pressuring an international technical body, the International Standards Organization. After the ISO's committee that deals with the issue received a draft standard for romanization of Cantonese script in 2019, Chinese delegates objected. Backers of the Cantonese standard pointed out that the languages are mutually unintelligible, and their writing scripts have diverged, especially after the mainland simplified characters during Mao's time. *The Wall Street Journal* described the Chinese efforts:

> An unusually large Chinese delegation followed with dozens of slides aggressively attacking the draft, unnerving some attendees, said three people familiar with the meeting. A Chinese delegation member told *The Wall Street Journal* that the proposed writing system is used only in Hong Kong and not by the 60 million Cantonese speakers elsewhere in China.[5]

The mainland contention ignores the millions of Cantonese speakers in Chinese communities around the world. Even if the language were used only by Hong Kong's 7.5 million people, the Chinese pushback conveys the message that a language with a rich tradition, especially in film and music, doesn't matter. How many millions more speakers are needed to matter? Hong Kong's population might represent a rounding error in China, but it is still larger than Singapore's, New Zealand's, or Ireland's. It is twice as large as the population of

Mongolia and more than ten times that of Bhutan or Luxembourg. In fact, more than one hundred countries have a population smaller than Hong Kong's. China's aim is clear: it wants to limit, if not eliminate, Cantonese identity.

The government is trying to build a sense of national identity among Hong Kongers with patriotic education in elementary schools. There is an opposing trend where so-called localists around the time of the 2014 Occupy Central movement started excluding mainland words from everyday speech. "If someone sees you using these words, you will be criticized heavily for being a Communist or mainlander," says Lau. "I am not a fan of this movement. I don't feel you can exclude external influence on language. Although I don't like this movement, this sense of ownership of language is growing among Hong Kongers."

I met Lau in 2015, a year after he'd started his dictionary project. Although the political situation has grown increasingly repressive, when we spoke in early 2021, he professed himself encouraged by the stronger sense of community and identity he saw emerging. "The atmosphere I feel is that everyone wants to build something in Hong Kong—painting, music, rappers, bands, and ViuTV, which is trying to build a TV station that feels like Hong Kong. This is not just about Cantonese." Indeed it is not.

My Cantonese teacher Chan is a polyglot who speaks a range of Asian languages, from Burmese to Japanese and from Korean to Thai. Born in 1991 and therefore too young to remember Hong Kong as a British colony, Chan doesn't see himself as mainland Chinese. "The culture I grew up in is very different from China. The things we eat, the festivals we celebrate—even if we celebrate the same Chinese New Year, we celebrate in different ways. For Chinese New Year, the northern Chinese eat water dumplings. We eat reddish rice cakes." Hong Kong celebrates Christmas and Easter as public holidays, unlike in the mainland. "Usually people associate Christmas as romantic, with the lights outside, a time to go out with your girlfriend or boyfriend. You don't have Christmas dinner at home. Restaurants will have expensive dinner packages."

For Chan and many in his generation, the high point of feeling

Chinese came at the time of the 2008 Beijing Olympics. "Many people were so proud of China. The opening and closing ceremonies gave you a new impression of China. The government distributed little flags to support China. At that time, you could find online discussion posts like 'I am so proud to be a Chinese person.' Hong Kong people who posted that want to delete it now." A scandal involving adulterated baby milk formula, which saw protesting parents of children who had been sickened by the milk punished more harshly than those who had adulterated the milk, was a turning point in Chan's perception of China. "All this kind of news wakened people around me. I knew China wasn't so developed, but I didn't have a bad impression. I knew they had rundown old towns and dirty toilets. Then, seeing the Chinese government, how they do these things [like the baby milk scandal]—that builds the Hong Kong identity, making Hong Kong people not want to admit they are Chinese."

The 2008 Sichuan earthquake, in the aftermath of which grief-stricken parents of some of the thousands of students who died because of shoddy school construction were harassed and detained following protests, became another milestone for Chan and his generation. "Most people my age would say 'I am from Hong Kong, not from China.' Many Chinese people see Hong Kong people and say, 'Ah, my brother!' (*Xiongdi, xiongdi!*). I think, 'Who are you? Who am I to you? Who are you to me?' I don't feel particularly connected to them." Despite Hong Kongers' best efforts, the Chinese government has succeeded in dividing them from their mainland compatriots. Mainlanders routinely disparage Hong Kong pro-democracy figures as "rubbish" and "dogs" who don't deserve to call themselves Chinese. "The average Hong Konger doesn't have close friends from China," says Chan. Ironically, a short-lived opening that allowed Chinese to take part in discussions on the Clubhouse media app in early 2021 provided Chan with a different vision of the mainland by allowing him to talk with like-minded mainlanders. One of the women in the group was crying as she spoke about her support for Hong Kong. "We don't know about that side of China," says Chan.

Signs of a Cantonese awakening notwithstanding, China's long-standing policy has been to suppress its peripheral regions, as it has in Tibet and Xinjiang. Xinjiang-style reeducation camps are unlikely to be seen in Hong Kong, but the insistence that foreign politicians cannot meet with Jimmy Lai or Martin Lee—just as they are told that they cannot meet with the Dalai Lama—has unsettling echoes of the way in which the pro-Tibetan movement was marginalized. More than 90 percent of Chinese are Han Chinese, said to be descended from the people in the Yellow River Basin, where China's first significant empire ruled two millennia ago. Han Chinese have been encouraged to move in large numbers to Tibet and Xinjiang, threatening these indigenous cultures. Although Cantonese are considered a subgroup of Han, something similar is at work in Hong Kong. More than one million mainland-born people have moved to Hong Kong since the 1990s, many traveling to the city under a so-called one-way permit immigration system over which Hong Kong has no control.[6] In an extreme case, a mainland arsonist who had torched a government building was expelled from Hong Kong but later readmitted to the territory under this scheme. Hong Kong had no power to exclude him.

Cities like Hong Kong need the best and the brightest to prosper. Hong Kong's future depends on attracting newcomers from the mainland, just as New York City lures many of America's, and the world's, most talented people. But Hong Kongers want to be able to continue to enjoy the high degree of autonomy they were promised. Instead, the mainland is doubling down on promoting a sense of Chinese national identity, with explicit patriotic education in schools and more cultural influence. A new generation is engaging with mainland media in a way that Chan and his peers do not. Many younger Hong Kongers are more open to Mandarin content online and to mainland Chinese culture. "I guess there will not be as much resistance as when we were students," says Chan. "Maybe they will just swallow what the teachers say," especially as they start to use Weibo, WeChat, and other mainland apps.

❀

Hong Kong has served above all as a business city, a fact frequently extolled in self-congratulatory announcements by both the colonial and the PRC government. Colonial administrators and the business elite prided themselves on the colony's low taxes, small government, and minimal bureaucracy. Possessing a free port facilitated Hong Kong's development as an entrepôt, where goods and people flowed through with ease, stimulating trade and economic growth. The cost came in stunted cultural, artistic, and educational development. As noted, education was neglected. Mandatory schooling, instituted in 1971, initially extended until the third grade; only in 1979 was a ninth-grade education required. The effect of this is still felt today. Anyone born before the mid-1960s attended either an elite private school or a church school (mostly Catholic or Protestant and a source for much of the strong Christian thread woven into Hong Kong), or went to no school at all. Many older people are functionally illiterate or have only a rudimentary education. University places were extremely limited, and few high school graduates matriculated before enrollments were expanded in the 1990s, thanks to reform efforts during the Patten governorship.

The 1990s and the first decade of the twenty-first century saw a cultural flowering in what had been a desiccated landscape. The first public library opened only in 1962, part of the new Bauhaus-inspired City Hall complex that also included a concert hall and the colony's first art museum. The visual arts scene was dominated by expatriates. As far as I can tell, there were no local Chinese painters who made a living from their work until the 1980s. Luis Chan, a Panamanian-born Cantonese whose hallucinatory style makes him the most famous of the first generation of Hong Kong–based painters, learned his technical skills through correspondence courses. Chan made his living selling shoes, working as a clerk, and, finally, as a commercial illustrator before achieving fame and a measure of material success later in his long life. (He died in 1995 at the age of ninety.)[7]

When I moved to Hong Kong in 1992, there were only a handful of commercial art galleries. One of the most prominent was founded by Alice King, the sister of Hong Kong's first post-handover chief executive, Tung Chee-hwa. King's Alisan Fine Arts championed Chinese expatriate artists such as Zao Wou-Ki, a Beijing-born artist who spent most of his life in Paris. The other significant gallery was Hanart TZ. Founder Johnson Chang (Chang

Tsong-zung) was a scholar who studied liberal arts with a focus on mathematics and philosophy at Williams College. He started out selling Chinese antiques and mixed a very contemporary artistic sensibility with a deep concern for the fate of Chinese civilization.

When I met Chang in the early 1990s, he was fresh from the success of a post-1989 show that Hanart had hosted with London's Marlborough Gallery, *China's New Art Post-1989*, a landmark post-Tiananmen effort that showcased a new generation of Chinese painters in Europe. Besides mainland artists, one of Chang's most important artists was the Taiwanese sculptor Ju Ming. Ju's sculptures, and paintings by many of the artists Hanart represented, were on display in the newly opened China Club. The China Club, mixing a 1930s Shanghainese décor with the Chinese paintings that Chang acquired, provided a lively pre-1997 alternative to places like the more sedate Hong Kong Club. A Chinese art scene was flourishing in the city before the handover, but Hong Kong artists themselves were almost invisible, mostly working in the shadows and exhibiting privately. Pioneers like King and Chang generally promoted mainland- or Taiwan-born Chinese painters who lived in China, Taiwan, or abroad. Galleries focused on the escapist fantasies of Luis Chan; or nonrepresentational works of Hong Kong Chinese-Australian painter Irene Chou; or traditional themes of women and flowers, such as in the bright acrylics of Chinese-American painter Walasse Ting[8]; or the abstractions of Zao Wou-Ki.

The gallery scene was confined to such a small circle of cognoscenti that, in order to draw more viewers, both King and Chang put on major shows not in their galleries but at the Hong Kong Arts Center in Wan Chai, part of an arts complex built in 1977 that was designed to provide an alternative venue to City Hall's limited arts facilities. From no venues in the early 1960s, through a slow building out of facilities like the art museum at City Hall in 1962 and the Arts Centre fifteen years later, to, in the late 1980s, a cultural complex that included a new venue for the art museum as well as two concert halls—the physical infrastructure for arts was slowly developing.

Even in the early 2000s, well after the handover, the local arts world was extremely limited. John Batten, an arts critic and longtime Hong Kong resident, organized the first Hong Kong ArtWalk in 2001. On that occasion, galleries threw open their doors, donating ticket proceeds to the Society for Community Organizations, an NGO that worked for the homeless. There were only about a dozen galleries in the early years of ArtWalk, all clustered in the area around the Mid-Levels escalator, just a five- or ten-minute walk from the heart of Central. So limited was the gallery scene that in one of those early years, I managed to visit almost all the participating galleries and still catch a performance of a Korean drumming group that was appearing as part of the Hong Kong Arts Festival. By the time ArtWalk ended in 2014, when a variety of fairs and other events made it superfluous, there were nearly one hundred galleries scattered around Hong Kong Island.

For most of the early 2000s, the arts remained something that most people in Hong Kong just didn't understand—unless an artwork had a big price tag attached. A front-page article in the *South China Morning Post* in 2006 derided a work by the noted French Chinese artist Sanyu as being little better than the sort of childish artwork a doting parent might tack up on the refrigerator.[9] (Sanyu's distinctive works later topped $20 million at auction.) When I was at the *Post*, a discussion at the daily news conference about a blockbuster French impressionist art show centered on the fact that the paintings were worth almost $600 million.[10] Suffice it to say there was no discussion of the art itself, let alone, say, of how it might have influenced Luis Chan or Walasse Ting.

Journalists weren't the only ones to cultivate this aggressive anti-intellectualism. A few evenings after our discussion of the show, at a dinner hosted by the French consul general at his residence on the Peak, the show's overseer told me, without any prompting on my part, that he could confirm the paintings in the show were in fact worth about $600 million. I've been to many art shows. Never before or since have I heard a show primarily referred to in monetary terms. Hong Kong seemed to be filled with people who, to quote Oscar Wilde, knew the price of everything and the value of nothing.

My cynicism notwithstanding, money provided much of the fuel for Hong Kong's art market to become one of the world's most important. In the early 2000s, Hong Kong went from being a minor outpost to the world's third most important auction market, after New York City and London. In arts as in finance, Hong Kong emerged in the 1990s and the early 2000s as the largest and most international Asian center. Auction houses Christie's and Sotheby's had long held semiannual auctions in Hong Kong that were Asia's largest, but the scale of their operations increased in the 2000s.

❧

At the turn of the century, the government announced plans for the West Kowloon Cultural District, billed as the world's biggest arts complex since Paris's Centre Pompidou opened in the early 1970s. It is, in fact, substantially larger than the Pompidou, arguably making it the world's largest-ever arts cluster. The nine-billion-dollar project, like most large-scale complexes, has been mired in controversy. It's costing more than three times the original budget and has endured a revolving door of top management, redrawn design concepts, and even changes in the selection of museums it would contain. It has also faced continuing political criticism related to the finances, the management, and, especially after the introduction of the National Security Law in 2020, the political content of the art.[11] Dissident Chinese artist Ai Weiwei's work—notably a photo where he raises his middle finger in Tiananmen Square—became a focus of the attacks. As censorship tightened, prospects for Hong Kong's future as an arts center waned.

The controversies reflect Hong Kong's political tensions. When Carrie Lam returned from Beijing to announce that the country's most prestigious museum, the Palace Museum, would open a branch at the site, the reaction was not one of joy and pride but of anger. The intense criticism that greeted the announcement, which was made without consultation and seemed akin to a gift bestowed by an emperor, reflected a deep antipathy toward the mainland.

Cantonese opera, with its elaborate costumes and stylized singing, is considered part of Hong Kong's cultural heritage, as UNESCO has recognized. It is still performed in a handful of Hong Kong theaters and now, more commonly, on temporary bamboo stages assembled in villages and on outlying islands for festivals. It is part of a larger tradition of Chinese opera. From a national perspective, it was understandable to showcase Chinese opera by naming the first building to open at the West Kowloon Cultural District the Xiqu Centre, *xiqu* being a Mandarin word. From a Hong Kong perspective, the use of Mandarin for a building that would showcase an important Cantonese art form was yet more evidence that Cantonese culture would be subsumed under, even smothered by, a larger "Chinese" culture. This homogenous culture would, with the exception of special displays by "ethnic minorities," be the Chinese Communist Party's version of culture. One of my Cantonese friends lamented that Cantonese are even worse off than the so-called ethnic minorities, as the former are also considered Han Chinese and therefore have no claim to any special identity.

The government knew that the class of international financiers it was wooing valued cultural attractions of the sort that London and New York City offered. So, it invested in hard physical infrastructure like the West Kowloon Cultural District. Less attention was given to the artists who would actually be showcased there. Edo de Waart, the Hong Kong Philharmonic's conductor in the early 2000s, noted the irony of spending billions of dollars on new concert halls while cutting the philharmonic orchestra's size, forcing him to fly in freelance musicians from the around the region to play at concerts. De Waart worried that there would not be enough performances to make use of the new concert venues; he lamented that the government was focusing on physical infrastructure while ignoring the underlying art, the artists, and the audiences.

At the same time, a new generation of artists was at work. In 1996, a group of seven artists founded Para Site, the city's first independent, artist-run venue. These artists were responding to the collective experience of Hong Kong, its decolonization, and its incorporation into the People's Republic of China. They also had more opportunity to study art, attend art shows, and produce artworks. Many more students were receiving arts education.[12]

In 2001, the Grotto Fine Art gallery opened, the first commercial gallery to focus solely on contemporary Hong Kong artists. A freer, more open society also engendered a different art scene. So, too, did an increasingly confrontational political situation. At the same time, the growing numbers of artists and art students found arts-related employment, especially with the development of the West Kowloon Cultural District.

Bouie Choi (Choi Yuk-kuen), one of the first artists showcased by Grotto, exemplifies these trends. She graduated from the Chinese University of Hong Kong in 2009—her student work was featured in one of Grotto's first shows—and then went to London, earning a master's from the Chelsea College of Art and Design at the University of London.[13] She later worked for six years as a community service worker for one of the city's largest charities, the St. James' Settlement, on a heritage preservation project, the colonial-era Blue House in Wan Chai. The job at the Blue House involved her in the community and gave her a deeper feeling for grassroots Hong Kong issues. In the years since Choi graduated from the Chinese University, her work has gone from meticulous, "carefully beautiful" paintings of insects and animals "with a fantasy-like ambience," in the words of critic John Batten, to something more hard-edged that mirrors the turbulent political times. Reflecting the 2019 protests and the subsequent pandemic restrictions, Choi's latest work is "violent and tender."[14] Choi is one of the better-known of the hundreds of Hong Kong artists whose work is now being shown in the city's more than one hundred art galleries. Many in this new generation of artists are politically engaged.

The Umbrella Movement gave Hong Kong's art world new creative energy. By 2019, artists had already developed a language of protest. One of the most provocative was Tiffany Sia's *Salty Wet* magazine. Pretending to be a softcore men's magazine, the work mixes photos of barely dressed models with cerebral intellectual snippets from French academics and Hong Kong artists, such as a picture of Samson Wong's 2014 pink neon work *Nothing we did could have saved Hong Kong[.] It was all wasted*. (Although Sia doesn't tell her English-speaking audience this, "salty wet," or *hàam sâp*, means "horny" in Cantonese.) To these, Sia adds her own take on China's destruction of Hong Kong, notably "Hong Kong is the world's first postmodern city to die." In a dig at the Chinese idea of integrating Hong Kong into the mainland by literally building bridges to connect it with the surrounding Pearl River Delta (the Greater Bay Area scheme), Sia proclaims that the "Pearl River Delta is the cunt of globalization." Sia's is challenging and unsettling work.

Sia's subsequent exhibition, *Too Salty Too Wet*, shown at Artists Space in New York City in 2021, wrestles with "how to uncover and recover narratives about trauma and violence, not only from the pro-democracy protests of the past few years, but from centuries of colonial subjugation." Her 2021 book, *Slippery When Wet*, aims, "to recover a sense of togetherness that is lost as some in the community stay while others go into exile or emigrate. What will this community look like on the diasporic road ahead?"[15] Artists are publicly engaging with the same issues that millions of ordinary Hong Kongers are grappling with: What happens when the way of life in what had been one of the freest and most vibrant places on earth is in danger of being extinguished? What happens, as is likely, when hundreds of thousands of people leave the city?

Stefani Kuo, a playwright born in Hong Kong in 1995, also spoke of this anguish in her 2021 play *Final Boarding Call*. Kuo started work on the play during the 2019 protests, and her characters grapple with what Hong Kong's future holds as their city is stifled. It is also worth underscoring how artists like these have incorporated international influences in their work and also brought Hong Kong to the attention of audiences abroad. Luis Chan learned of international trends through correspondence school courses and the occasional exhibition in Hong Kong. Sia was born in Hong Kong but grew up in the United States. Kuo moved to the United States for boarding school and is now studying at Yale. Choi studied in London.

In strikingly different ways, the work of Choi, Sia, Kuo, and many of their peers reflects the violence and chaos of recent years. These artists are pioneers. When they were born, in the 1990s, around the time of the colonial handover, Hong Kong had only a meager art world. Its development in a generation, founded on prosperity and forged by politics, has transformed how Hong Kongers see their city.

Choi, Sia, Kuo, and their generation have no precedent. Hong Kong as we know it is being snuffed out. These artists and many others want to ensure it is not forgotten.

❦

Film is perhaps the quintessential Hong Kong art form. Film loves the city. Its neon lights, narrow streets, and tall buildings, its striking harbor and steep mountains, make Hong Kong an urban cinematographer's dream. Moviemaking in Hong Kong took off in the 1950s, after the Communist takeover of China wrecked the industry in Shanghai. There was a nervous energy to many Hong Kong movies during the second half of the twentieth century, even though most of them were fairly predictable crime or love stories. Something about the frisson of a very cinematic city imprinted itself on even mediocre movies.

As it did with painting, politics has shaped Hong Kong films in ways that are both obvious and subtle. With the erasure of cosmopolitan Shanghai in 1949, Hong Kong assumed the mantle of the most urban, modern Chinese society. From the 1950s through the 1970s, a genre of Hong Kong–produced movies portrayed the colony as a modern, prosperous capitalist society. Women in Hong Kong movies were shown as educated, often with ambitions beyond the home. This wasn't an accidental portrayal. As part of a Cold War propaganda effort to highlight the contrast between prosperous, modern Hong Kong and the drab Communist People's Republic, the Asia Pictures studio even accepted funding from a CIA-linked organization, the money enabling it to project a vision of how the Chinese-speaking world saw Hong Kong.[16]

Both mainland China and Taiwan were preoccupied by internal politics and nation-building, so Hong Kong films had little competition in export markets. Remarkably, it was claimed that for many years Hong Kong was the world's second- or third-largest film exporter, trailing only the United States and India. (This assertion is made in many discussions of Hong Kong cinema, although I have not been able to find original data to support the claim.) Films made by Cathay Studios and Shaw Studios were the most important part of a Cantonese wave that washed over Chinese diaspora communities in Southeast Asia and beyond in the 1950s and '60s.[17]

Audiences in the West took note of Hong Kong movies, particularly Bruce Lee's martial arts pictures of the 1970s. (Lee first showed his kicks as Kato in the short-lived 1966–67 *Green Hornet* television series, then acted in more than a half dozen movies before his premature death during filming in Hong Kong in 1973.) Born in San Francisco's Chinatown Hospital and raised largely in Hong Kong, Lee changed the image of Hong Kong and of Hong Kong films, both internationally and within Hong Kong itself. His movies, distributed on videocassettes that in the West were sold mostly in Chinatown stores, became underground classics. In fight scenes like that in Rome's Colosseum with Chuck Norris (in *The Way of the Dragon*, Norris's film debut), Lee showed Western audiences that Chinese actors were more than submissive Charlie Chans, that Chinese could and would fight back. In *The Way of the Dragon*, Lee's character successfully fights the Mafia, a sniper, a Japanese martial artist, and a turncoat within the ranks of the Chinese restaurant workers he is defending, as well as Norris's character. He shows quite literally that Chinese couldn't be kicked around anymore.[18]

When dictionary editor Lau Chaak-ming talks about "making Cantonese great again," he is thinking about this golden age from the 1950s through the 1980s, when tiny Hong Kong was one of the world's largest film exporters. Hong Kongers boasted that "Wherever there are Chinese, there are Hong Kong movies."[19] Hong Kong revealed, if only cinematically, how a free, modern Chinese society could operate.

Mainland China's cinematic opening in the 1990s prompted a crisis from which Hong Kong's cinema has never recovered. China started producing its own export-quality films, and at the same time, Hong Kong filmmakers were asked to tailor—self-censor—their films for the mainland market. For instance, the ending was altered in the Mandarin-language version of *Infernal Affairs*, one of the greatest Hong Kong movies ever made and the model for Martin Scorsese's Oscar-winning *The Departed*. (The original 2002 movie was in Cantonese, but as is common, a Mandarin-dubbed version was also produced.)

In the Cantonese Hong Kong version, the undercover cop (played by Tony Leung) is killed by a mole within the force who is then killed by yet another mole (played by Andy Lau). In the mainland version, the honest Leung lives while the crooked Lau is killed. *Infernal Affairs* was released in 2002. The demands for political orthodoxy would intensify in the coming decades.

Within the past decade, Hong Kong's cinema has become explicitly political. The most important film is *Ten Years*. I discussed earlier (chapter 3) the film's controversial debut—the blackout by the mainland television broadcaster CCTV of the Hong Kong Film Festival awards ceremony, an attack by the head of the Hong Kong Tourism Board, and an abrupt end to cinema showings. Unofficial public viewings took place when cinemas refused to show the movie.

Ten Years is composed of five short films of about twenty minutes each. Each was shot by a different director, and the shorts bear no obvious relationship to one another except in that they each portray a filmmaker's artistic vision of Hong Kong ten years hence, in 2025. The short films range from the provocative to the elegiac. In the first (*Extras*), mainland operatives in Hong Kong stage a terrorist shooting in order to stoke antiforeign, racist sentiments and pave the way for passage of a national security law. With the 2020 passage of the National Security Law, following a period of political turmoil, this seems uncomfortably close to the truth. (Coincidentally, *Extras* is set in 2020.) In the short, the primary would-be assassin (who is ultimately killed by police) is a South Asian; in 2019, pro-democracy campaigner Jimmy Sham was attacked by South Asian assailants. South Asians occupy an important part of Hong Kong; although there have been South Asians living there since the founding of the colony, they are subject to ongoing discrimination and are well represented in criminal activities. The use of South Asians as muscle to attack pro-democracy forces is common.

The fourth short, *Self-immolator,* shows an elderly woman staging an act of self-immolation in protest against mainland China. (This segment particularly irked Beijing.) *Dialect* portrays a taxi driver who fails to master Mandarin and is prohibited from picking up passengers at popular tourist destinations. In the end, he cannot communicate even with his school-age daughter, whose lessons are in Mandarin. *Local Egg* recounts the story of a shopkeeper as he tries to unearth what is behind the planned closure of the last local egg producer in Hong Kong. Simultaneously, he needs to cope with his radical Red Guard–like student son, who terrorizes bookstore owners who sell dissident material. (There is a happy ending: the son is a double agent who, in reality, is giving the booksellers advance warning of the raids.) *Season of the End* is the most poetic—and perhaps the most puzzling. A couple, played by Wong Ching and Lau Ho-chi, meticulously and systematically preserves objects from homes set to be destroyed by bulldozers, as if they are preserving archeological fragments or laboratory specimens. As their work nears an end, Lau's character conceives of his own body as the final piece. The segment ends with Wong's character scraping away Lau's skin, reducing him to a specimen.

All the shorts in *Ten Years* are connected by the themes of loss, of the desire to preserve a Hong Kong that is being crushed under the onslaught of the mainland. In *Extras* and *Self-immolator,* political violence portends a grim future. *Dialect* portrays the destruction of Cantonese language and, with it, a way of life. *Season of the End* is a sad and extended meditation on the loss of culture. *Local Egg* contains elements of political violence and the destruction of traditional culture.

What was perhaps more remarkable than the film itself was the reaction from the pro-Beijing establishment in Hong Kong and on the mainland. The chauvinistic *Global Times* accused the film's directors of trying to "scare the public in Hong Kong and spread anxiety" and urged them to "think what consequences this will bring to Hong Kong."[20] The film was released in 2015, just as the five Causeway Bay Bookstore / Mighty Currents booksellers were abducted by Chinese agents, thus substantiating the fears expressed in the movie. By 2020, much of what the movie had prefigured had come to pass; thankfully, self-immolation had not. The future shown in *Ten Years* had, some Hong Kongers joked sardonically, arrived five years early.

Ten Years was not the only movie to capture the feeling of a Hong Kong under threat. An ultra-short seven-minute video released on YouTube in early 2014, six months before the start of the Occupy Central protests, explored similar themes. The plot of *Hong Kong Will Be*

Destroyed After 33 Years centers on a fictional 2014 announcement that a meteorite will destroy Hong Kong in 2047 (the year when Hong Kong's fifty years of promised autonomy under the "one country, two systems" arrangement would terminate).

In the film, the central government and business interests build a new Hong Kong in "northwestern China" (Xinjiang) and move the stock exchange, the airport, the I. M. Pei–designed Bank of China Tower, and much of the territory's business to the new city. Two-thirds of Hong Kongers move to the new site. For those who stay in the city, Hong Kong over the next decade returns to a past golden age. There are no more shopping malls and no stock exchange, but small businesses thrive. There are no gray-market traders from the mainland—a common complaint for more than a decade has been the thousands of mainlanders who buy up large quantities of goods in Hong Kong for resale across the border—but renewed interest in Hong Kong by foreign tourists. A general election is quickly held.

The seven-minute film logged six hundred thousand views in less than a month after its release in March 2014. With characteristic hypersensitivity, China's State Council Information Office (the cabinet's communication department) banned any positive mentions of the movie (in "video, text, etc."), which it objected to on the grounds that it featured Hong Kongers "saving themselves." This response to a short, low-budget YouTube video—a platform that is banned in China—showed an almost pathological determination to smother free expression. As one of the film's creators, Yik Kan-cheung, told *The Diplomat*, "China is trying to suffocate Hong Kong."[21]

From the modern affluence of the 1950s to Bruce Lee's ferocious martial arts to the more directly engaged cinema of 2014 and beyond, Hong Kong's movies have always had political aspects, whether covert or overt. Recent decades have seen a notable uptick in the number of these edgier, harder-hitting, and more politically engaged Hong Kong filmmakers. Recent events have also prompted Beijing to take a more punitive and assertive approach toward movies, and the directors and actors who make them, that it doesn't like.

With the introduction of the National Security Law (NSL) in 2020, the quest for a Hong Kong identity has entered a new phase.